MYTH

Myth

A Biography of Belief

DAVID LEEMING

OXFORD
UNIVERSITY PRESS

2002

OXFORD
UNIVERSITY PRESS

Oxford   New York

Athens   Auckland   Bangkok   Bogotá   Buenos Aires   Cape Town   Chennai
Dar es Salaam   Delhi   Florence   Hong Kong   Istanbul   Karachi   Kolkata
Kuala Lumpur   Madrid   Melbourne   Mexico City   Mumbai   Nairobi   Paris
São Paulo   Shanghai   Singapore   Taipei   Tokyo   Toronto   Warsaw

and associated companies in
Berlin   Ibadan

Published by Oxford University Press, Inc.
198 Madison Avenue, New York, New York 10016

Oxford is a registered trademark of Oxford University Press

Library of Congress Cataloging-in-Publication Data
Leeming, David Adams, 1937—
Myth: a biography of belief / David Leeming
p. cm.   Includes bibliographical references and index.
ISBN 0-19-514288-8
1. Mytholgoy.
I. Title.
BL311.L324 2001
291.1'3—dc21   2001032940

Book design by Adam B. Bohannon

9   8   7   6   5   4   3   2   1
Printed in theUnited States of America
on acid-free paper

For James & Pamela Morton

Contents

Preface ~~

This book is based on a series of lectures delivered at the Interfaith Center of New York in the fall of 2000. Each of the essays opens with a selection of primarily traditional myths from various cultures. These are intended to bring the reader directly into the world of mythology—to set a mood, as it were. I then move on to definitions of the pattern or archetype revealed in the given myths. The next step involves interpretation of the archetype and its function and includes a number of fictional situations such as a gathering of myth-makers from many cultures and eras and the psycho-analysis of a personified culture. Literary examples are included in each essay to illustrate the remolding of old myths and the emergence of new ones.

There are those who will be offended by the treatment of religious stories as "myths," whereas others will recognize in my approach an attempt to move beyond narrow sectarian and exclusive understandings on the one hand and blindness to spiritual issues on the other. Myths reflect our spiritual and psychological development, our spiritual and psychological biography as a species, and it seems fair to hope that religions can also reflect that development.

The first essay is an introductory exploration of the whole relationship between myth and religion. It suggests that a comparative approach to religious narratives—cultural dreams—can lead to a broader understanding of who we are and where we are going. The second essay treats a universal story, the creation myth, in many culturally revealing forms and suggests a new creation myth as reflected in both science and the phenomenon of modernism and postmodernism. The third essay is concerned with the difficult question of divinity, especially as it reflects the question of gender in human history. The fourth essay approaches the hero myth by way of a version of Joseph Campbell's monomyth and the relationship between psyche and soul, ending with a consideration of the strangely ubiquitous human thirst for union with something out of reach.

MYTH

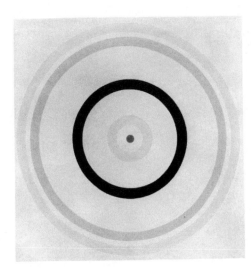

CHAPTER I

Introduction

Myth and Religion

"It is through symbol that man finds his way out of his particular situation and opens himself to the general and universal."

MIRCEA ELIADE

Five "Religious" Myths

Judaism

Happy are you, Israel, peerless, set free!
The Lord is the shield that guards you,
the Blessed One is your glorious sword.
When your enemies come cringing to you,
you will trample their backs under foot.

Deuteronomy 33:29

Islam

There is no God but Allah, and Muhammad is his Messenger.

The First Pillar of Islam

Christianity

God raised him to the heights and bestowed on him the name above all names, that at the name of Jesus every knee should bow—in heaven, on earth, and in the depths.

Paul, Philippians 2:9–10

Zen Buddhism

Nirvana is here and Now, in the midst of Samsara. . . . A wise man will see Nirvana at once in the ordinary things of life. . . . When master Tung-shan was asked "What is the Buddha?" he replied, "Three pounds of flax."

Watts, *The Spirit of Zen*, 30

Moses and the Shepherd

Once Moses overheard a shepherd talking. It sounded as if the shepherd were talking to an uncle or a friend, but he was talking to God.

"I would like to help you, wherever you are, wash your clothes, pick lice from you, kiss your hands and feet at bedtime. All I can say, recalling you, is *ahhhhhhh-hhhhh* and *ayyyyyyyy!*"

Moses was very upset. "Are you talking in such a way to the very creator of heaven and earth? Don't you have more respect?"

The shepherd hung his head and wandered off, saddened. But God came to rebuke Moses, saying:

What's wrong for one person is right for another,
Your poison can be someone else's honey.
I don't care about purity or diligence in worship.
Or impurity and sloth.
They mean nothing to me. I am above all that.
One way of worshipping is as good as another.
Hindus do Hindu things.
Muslims in India do what they do.

It is all praise, and it is all right.
I don't listen to the words the worshippers say.
I look inside for humility. That's reality.
Mere language, phraseology, isn't reality.
I want burning, burning!
Be friends, all of you, with your burning.
Burn your thinking in humility.
Burn your phrases.

Celaladin Rumi

Myth Types

Three general types of myth have been central to human societies and continue to influence the way we think, speak, and act today. *Creation* myths tell us where we came from, how things began. They are our primary myths, the first stage in what might be called the psychic life of the species. Creation is almost always linked to the concept of *Deity*, one of the strongest but most corruptible expressions of our collective being. Deities are metaphors for—dreams of—our ultimate progenitors, and psychology has taught us how important our mental depictions and memories of our parents are to any real understanding of our own identities. The story of the *Hero* is the most human and overtly psychological of the dominant myth patterns. Hero stories can be said to be metaphors for our personal and collective progress through life and history. Creation, Deity, and Hero all seem to lead inevitably to that very strangest and most mystical expression of the human imagination, the concept of union, which, depending upon era and tradition, has been called by many names, of which nirvana, individuation, self-identity, and wholeness are a few.

We commonly use the word "myth" to mean a generally held belief or concept that is clearly untrue or merely fanciful. It is a myth that crime never pays, that George Washington never told a lie, that all women are intuitive, or that walking under a ladder brings bad luck. This definition of myth as false belief or superstition develops naturally enough from the more accurate understanding of the word as a fabulous and obviously untrue narrative of the deeds of heroes and gods—characters such as Odin or Pallas Athena or the Native American Trickster. But whereas common usage myths of the under the ladder sort are for the most part products of the secular world, mythic narratives are the sacred stories of religions.

All cultures and religions have sacred stories that the common sense of people in other cultures and religions recognizes as myths. The carrying off of the maiden Persephone by the god Hades is a fanciful and untrue story of someone else's religion. We call that story a myth. It is difficult to believe that the Buddha was conceived in a dream by a white elephant, so we call that story a myth as well. But, of course, stories such as the parting of the Red Sea for the fleeing Hebrews, Muhammad's Night Journey, and the dead Jesus rising from the tomb are just as clearly irrational narratives to which a Hindu or a Buddhist might understandably apply the word "myth." All of these stories are definable as myths because they contain events that contradict both our intellectual and physical experience of reality. But since stories of the ancient Hebrews and Jesus are central to "our" monotheistic religions we tend to resist labeling them as myths. Religious people have always assumed that their sacred stories are both unique and different from myths. Not only the rabbi, the imam, and the priest, but the Hindu holy man, the Navajo shaman, and the Dogon animist will invariably say that the stories of his or her religion are in many cases historical and certainly the vessels of eternal truth.

Certain lay thinkers—Carl Jung, Mircea Eliade, and Joseph Campbell are three of the best known—have suggested that both definitions of myth, as illusory stories and as containers of eternal truth, are valid simultaneously. For these thinkers, the great sacred stories are products of the imagination, but are nevertheless in some sense true in ways that history cannot be. Eliade emphasizes that so-called myths are regarded by believers as "true history" because they are always concerned with "realities." The emergence creation story of the Hopis is a "myth" in the common usage sense. It cannot be *true* because it is outside our human experience. Yet the Hopi are there on their mesas in what we call Arizona, and their lives are centered in the reality of their myth; in fact, their self-identity is dependent on it. That is, the Hopi creation myth expresses the reason for being, the sacred mana without which the Hopi do not exist. The Hopi are literally energized in the present time by their myth. In any case, Eliade would say, what is false about a belief that we are children of the Earth, that we emerged from the Mother of being?

Jung and Campbell take a more specifically psychological approach; for them, myths are comparable to dreams and should be regarded as seriously as we regard dreams. Myths provide direct insight to the collective psyche or the collective soul, and to repress or dismiss them as mere illusion is psychologically and spiritually harmful. Dreams provide us with important information about ourselves—information uncorrupted by conscious defense mechanisms. Myths do the same thing for cultures. In short, say Jung and Campbell, we need myths—those of our individual and cultural past and origins—and a mythical consciousness in the present time, to show us who we are, self-knowledge and identity having to do with intangibles that transcend mere name, parentage, and geographical location.

Eliade, Jung, Campbell, and others who take myths seriously as vehicles for truth almost always do so as universalists or comparatists. At the level of the archetypes revealed by comparison—the universal psychic tendencies that result in such ubiquitous themes as creation, the descent to the underworld, the concept of divinity, and the hero quest—mythologies may be said to be the dreams of humanity, products of what Jung called the "collective unconscious." At the very least, the archetypal images become the basis for a kind of universal symbolic language, through which, as Thomas Merton puts it, "we are summoned to [a] new awareness . . . of the inner meaning of life and reality itself" (Merton, 1,2,11).

It might be said that for the comparatist, the truth of a story such as the resurrection of Jesus becomes evident only when it is compared to other stories of the resurrection, such as those of Osiris or Persephone, and in that comparison is freed from the restrictions of the merely local or the merely sectarian. According to this view, the real importance of the resurrection myth, whether or not it is based in some sort of historical fact, lies in resurrection and not in the individuals who are resurrected. "Symbols," as Heinrich Zimmer suggested, "hold the mind to truth but are not themselves the truth" (Campbell, *Masks* 4: 625). The point is that when we discover through comparison that resurrection and virgin birth, for instance, are not the private property of Christians or that covenants with God are not peculiar to Jews, we are faced with something that transcends the literal interpretations of so many so-called fundamentalists and are freed to appreciate a human truth that is larger than our particular cultural truth. Instead of focusing on the historicity and literal truth of all aspects of Jesus's life, for instance, we can finally consider the *reality* of resurrection and virgin birth. As a Zen master once said to me, "The first step of Zen is to kill the Buddha."

Without direction, the comparative approach is one that occurs to the strict "believer," if at all, usually in the context of a confrontation with a significant modern dilemma. The dilemma in question is particularly acute for a religion that stresses its exclusivity, that preaches the literal and historical rather than the symbolic truth of its myths, that presents itself as the only earthly embodiment of eternal truth, as *the* "way." The dilemma grows out of the conflict between the scientific-rationalist training that is the basis for our everyday experience of the world and the mythic and ritualistic experience that is central to any given religious tradition. From a very early age the individual learns the importance of being rational. Yet the very essence of myth and ritual is anti-rational. Life in our temples and rituals, in the physical and psychological space we designate as temporarily or permanently holy, is radically different from life in the "real" world. In ritual or liturgical space we deal with the mystery behind life and we act uncharacteristically—we sing what we could speak, we wear costumes, we assume unusual postures, we imitate the actions of mythic ancestors—and we celebrate events that are clearly impossible according to the laws of reason. At some level the young believer is aware of the discrepancy, and the discrepancy must inevitably be disturbing, especially if no vehicle is provided for the assimilation of the myth and ritual into the world of rational experience. The student learns that one and one always equal two, that an object in a vacuum always accelerates at a particular speed, that reproduction depends on a particular coincidence of events, and that death is the negation of particular life, but when that same student enters the religious space of his or her tradition and is told that Yahweh spoke to Moses from a burning bush, that Mary became pregnant with Jesus without "knowing" a man, or that spirits are alive and well in trees, the student's psyche has to adjust in some way to this contradictory set of messages or risk a kind of social schizophrenia.

One way to adjust is simply to deny the validity of the religious beliefs or at least to de-mythologize and de-ritualize them. Ritual postures and actions can be eschewed as unnecessary absurdities and the wisdom of prophets and culture heroes can take precedence over any supposedly miraculous events of the distant past or ancient claims to godhead. Most religions contain "reformist" wings that represent this point of view. Another approach is to accept the sacred stories literally, with or without the assistance of complex ritual, and to become what is called a fundamentalist. The phenomenon of fundamentalism has always been with us and is particularly prevalent today.

Still another answer to the problem is the comparative approach mentioned earlier. To make this comparative leap out of religious or mythic exclusivity is not to deny the validity of one's own sacred stories, but rather it is to see their universality as truthful metaphors and to relate them to our current level of knowledge and experience. This kind of ecumenism does not require the giving up of the rituals or the sacred space of one's culture or religion. It is surely unrealistic, in any case, to attempt to create a world religion, as one does not worship archetypes but cultural embodiments of archetypes. In fact, the universal language of myth and archetype *requires* the elements of particular cultural experience in order to be realized, just as dreams require the local experience of individuals. Sectarian myths and rituals, as identifying cultural actions, are important for the establishment of cultural identity and a *state of awe* without which there is little chance for the knowledge contained in the mythic sphere to affect our lives. In ritual that "works," the barriers of rationalism are at least momentarily broken down, allowing the emotional experience of the reality and truth of divine incarnation, godly covenants, or death and rebirth embodied in *but by no means restricted to* our own cultural myths. The fact that Christian ritual celebrates the incarnation of the Unknown in Jesus, while Hindu ritual celebrates it very differently but apparently at least as effectively in Śiva, Viṣṇu, or the Goddess, is a mystery that becomes acceptable and just according to what might be called "God logic" as opposed to human logic. More important is the fact that all cultures are joined in their many different ways in the great "religious" and mythological process of examining the Unknown. Together we are all doing what Thomas Berry suggests is the defining human act of making creation conscious of itself, the act that differentiates us from other species and is perhaps our reason for being. To put it another way, if the emergence myth defines and energizes the Hopi as Hopi, the very existence of myth and ritual defines us all as a species.

William Doty, in defining the words *myth* and *mythology*, suggests a connection between the universal *ma*, the sound a baby makes at its mother's breast, which is also the Indo-European root for *mother*, and the root sound *mu* out of which emerges the Greek word *mythos*, literally "to make a sound with the mouth" or "word." This *ma-mu* connection he calls "mother-myth," which we might also call the beginning word, the first stage in the articulation of creation. Doty traces the development of the *mythos* word to its Homeric meaning first as style and then as the arrangement of words in story form, then to Plato as a metaphorical tale used to explain realities beyond the power of simple logic—such as the famous myth of the cave—and finally to Aristotle's use of the term as that most important of dramatic elements, "plot," the significant arrangement of events for the ritual process that was Greek tragedy (2–3). Mythology or *mythologia* is a combination of *mythos* and *logos*, or informing principle, later the "Word" of the Christian creation myth of John, which begins "In the beginning was the Word." To study mythology is to study myth-logic in general, or the defining myths of cultures in particular, or the cultural and collective inner life of the human quest for self-identity that stretches back at least to the Paleolithic cave paintings, themselves expressions of our defining drive to make a metaphor, to "tell a story," a drive that continues into the present.

Myth Today

Mythologists are always asked about myth *today*. If mythical consciousness and myth-making are so important to our individual and collective beings, how do the old myths operate now, and where are today's myths, today's myth-making, and today's myth-makers? Or have we become so mastered by our so-called scientific-rationalistic aspect that we can no longer take seriously anything beyond its scope?

The first point to recognize is that for the most part we do not consciously invent myths *as* myths any more than we consciously create dreams. There are, of course, consciously created philosophical narratives used to explain inexplicable mysteries, Plato's cave myth being one. Modern science uses "thought experiments" in a similar manner. Here, for instance, is physicist Erwin Schrödinger's (1887–1961) famous Cat in the Box experiment:

> In a box there is some radioactive material, an atom of which has a 50 percent chance of decaying in a set time and being recorded by a detector. There is also a live cat and a container of poison in the box. If the atom decay does not occur, the container will break and the cat will die. There is seemingly a 50 percent chance that after a certain time the cat in the box will be dead. So, we know after a while that the cat is either dead or alive. But, in the world of Quantum Mechanics this logic does not apply. According to that world, the cat cannot be either dead or alive until we actually open the box to see what has happened. Only through conscious observation does anything become real. (see Gribbon, 2–3)

And there is Einstein's space-traveling Relativity Twin Paradox:

> There were two twins. One went on a round trip into outer space. When he got back home he was

younger than his brother, because his heart, brain, and bloodflow "clocks" had slowed down during the trip. This is because time has a material or "length" aspect. The space twin was surprised on his return to discover how much older his brother was. (see Capra, 170)

Still another good example of such a myth is Nobel Prize winner Alfred Gilman's description of G proteins, in which aspects of cellular activity are treated as conscious beings:

Cells need to *know* . . . most of the agents convey *information* through intermediaries. They issue *orders* . . . relay the *information* to a series of intercellular *middlemen* that ultimately pass the *orders* to the final executors. (quoted in Artigas, 97–98)

It is not surprising that a science fiction writer such as Madeleine L'Engle should seize upon such narratives for the much-loved young adult series that includes *A Wrinkle in Time*, *A Wind in the Door*, *A Swiftly Tilting Planet*, and *Many Waters*, in the second of which, for instance, the setting for an exciting struggle for survival is the cellular world of the human bloodstream.

But, for the most part, myths are created by the collective imagination as metaphorical projections of the way things are in life. Myths emerge from our experience of reality, from our instinctive need to clothe that experience in mimetic story and concept. It is also true that as our experience as cultures and as a species changes, so do our myths. Old myths (and related rituals) grow and new ones are born so that we can step out of our merely material lives and project onto a screen, as it were, our relation to the whole picture of existence. Again, it could well be that to repress this growth and this birth is as damaging to the culture and the species as the analogous repression of the dream messages of the psyche would be to the individual.

THE CHALLENGE TO RELIGION

Traditionally, religions have been the repositories and interpreters of sacred stories—of myths—and the creators of rituals to express them. But as religions become institutionalized or associated with secular political power, these collective sacred metaphors and the religions themselves tend to be distorted for self-serving or political purposes. One need only look at recent events in the Middle East, in India, in Indonesia, in the Sudan, in Sri Lanka, or in Northern Ireland, to mention only a few examples of the politicized misuse of religion. Historically, the phenomenon in question has by no means been limited to extremist fringes or extremist religions. The history of mainstream Christianity, for example, contains glaring examples of repression: of the feminine principle embodied in Mary and the Holy Spirit, of the Jewishness of Jesus, of the "truth" revealed in the apocryphal gospels, of the essential message of peace conveyed by Jesus himself, and of the human mind's natural need to interpret its intellectual and physical enviroment. The distortions of fundamentalism are, of course, more obvious and more marked by literal interpretations for political purposes. The militant self-righteousness of fundamentalist Christianity and of fundamentalist Islam and Judaism, too, are clearly in contrast to the tolerance expressed in the New Testament, the Qur'an, and the Torah and in the compassionate teachings of the founders and prophets of the Abrahamic religions. If we think of religiosity as an aspect of our quest for psychological wholeness, the misuse of religious myth is analogous to a conscious editing of our dreams or a denial of their real metaphorical meaning in order to deceive ourselves and those around us. In the process we block the path to enlightenment. Historically, as cultures, we have done just that, misinterpreting our myths to justify, for example, arguments for gender and racial superiority and economic privilege, thus precluding *social* wholeness.

The problem facing religions is not only the perversion of existing myths and traditions but the repression of new revelations. With the exception of some forward-looking factions, religions around the world today all too often not only still claim to be the sole repositories of eternal truth but repress or resist the messages of the myths that are emerging in our time. Religions are said to be timeless, by which too many religious people often really mean unchanging. Individuals grow, cultures develop, knowledge and horizons are expanded, but institutionalized religions often resist development, failing to realize that it is not the religious system or the culture it represents that is sacrosanct but the continuing growth in human consciousness it should be nurturing. As Mark Schorer has said, "Myths are the instruments by which we *continually* struggle to make our experience intelligible to ourselves" (Doty, 10).

When that *continuing* process is forgotten or denied, the function of religions is taken over by others. Sometimes this is healthy and natural, sometimes it is not. Myths can be appropriated and tampered with by individuals and societies who pass off metaphor as fact, attempt to turn myth into history or history into myth and who even create ritual systems to provide the awe and wonder that bring myth to life. American "robber barons" of the nineteenth century played havoc with the myth of predestination as did the formulators of the doctrine of Manifest Destiny with the myths of Eden and the Messiah. Twentieth-century Western totalitarianism in its various forms owed much to the messianic and utopian aspects central to the Judeo-Christian tradition and created de facto religious systems, complete with ritual and dogma to support the artificially created myths in question. Communism, dominated by the "trinity" of Marx, Engles, and Lenin, promised a utopia based on a communal bonding that would not have surprised or offended early Christians. Military parades before the assembled leaders on the balcony above Red Square took on the aura of religious ritual. In China the cult of Mao included myths of the leader's almost superhuman intellectual and physical power. In Hitler's Germany, too, the *Führer* was glorified as a culture hero, and the justification for German dominance owed much to ancient myths such as those contained in the *Niebelungenlied* and the operas of Wagner. In mass meetings surrounded by the mythic symbols of National Symbolism the Hitler Youth expressed devotion to their hero in a style that suggested religious fanaticism rather than political loyalty.

If religions merely cling to "fundamental" past understandings, denying revelations at hand, they will, of course, become superfluous. By not allowing myths to grow and develop, by denying new prophecy, as it were, many religious entities contribute to stultification and even collective psychic unbalance. It is as if they insisted that adolescent dreams were the sole vehicles for truth and took a pill to stop further dreaming.

This is not to say that there are no religious people

paying attention to current revelations in such areas as science and gender roles. There are, as indicated earlier, religious communities struggling to reconfigure old liturgies, dogmas, and traditions in light of new knowledge and understanding—in light of the emerging planetary or ecological mythology discussed below. In fact, there have always been visionaries capable of seeing beyond the sectarian and literal barriers of their time. The Buddha was one, as were Jesus and Muhammad. There have always been theologians and religious devotees who have shared the open-mindedness of these prophetic figures. Mystics of all the great religions have especially been in agreement about their own traditions being non-exclusive vessels for the eternal and continuing process of making creation conscious of itself. To quote the great Islamic Sufi mystic Celaladin Rumi (c. 1207–1273), the founder of the "Whirling Dervishes," "There are many lamps/ But the light is the same."

A New Mythology?

Naturally, it is difficult to recognize myths as they emerge from the cultural and collective psyches. It is easy enough to look at a picture on a wall and to analyze its component parts, just as we have no difficulty studying the myths of Greece and Egypt. But to analyze the picture from within, as one of its parts, is problematic. This is true enough when we talk about our own ancient religious "myths." It is even more true when we speak of those myths currently developing around us and expressed not only in narratives but perhaps in such areas as ecological, earth-centered rather than monumental architecture, the repetitive "mysticism" of postmodernist painting and music, and religious and, albeit isolated, sociopolitical beliefs and practices that tend toward inclusiveness rather than exclusiveness.

Perhaps the best indication of the beginnings of the acceptance of a new mythology is the relatively recent recognition of the common purposes and understandings of the old enemies, religion and science, spirit and reason. At the progressive fringes of even mainline religious traditions we now find people who not only no longer speak of our patriarchal right as a species to conquer nature and rule the world but rather of the importance of human consciousness as a functional aspect of earth and of creation itself. These people are concerned with better understanding the myth of God in light of our deeper understanding from physics and biology of the interrelatedness of all aspects of creation. Scientists like Lewis Thomas and James Lovelock, Paul Davies, Lynn Margulis and Fred Hoyle, for instance, and religious thinkers like Thomas Merton, Thomas Berry, and Matthew Fox all point to our being a functioning part of an interrelated Gaian universe. To the extent that this new realization—this emerging narrative of inter-connectedness as opposed to dominance and exclusiv-ity—takes hold, people will necessarily look at politics, nationalism, gender roles, economics, race, moral val-ues, art, education, religion—at everything—in a new way. In light of this new myth, the old religious systems that once stressed the importance of revelation for their own communities may well take on a more planetary, ecological, nurturing, more feminine dimension. It is to the emergence of the new mythology that the balance of this book is devoted.

CHAPTER II

Creation

Myth, Science, and Modernism

"Our emergent cosmos is the fundamental context for all discussions of value, meaning, purpose, or ultimacy of any sort."

THOMAS BERRY

AND BRIAN SWIMME

Bill Jacobson, *Yolk*. Courtesy A/D, New York.

Six Creation Myths

The Zuni Creation

In the fourfold womb of the world, all terrestrial life was conceived from the lying together of Earth Mother and Sky Father upon the world waters. Earth Mother grew large with so great a number of progeny. She pushed Sky Father away from her and began to sink into the world waters, fearing that evil might befall her offspring, just as mothers always fear for their firstborn before they come forth. Unnerved by this foreboding, she kept her offspring unborn within her and discussed her fears with Sky Father. Together, they wondered how, even in the light of the sun, these offspring would know one place from another. Changeable as are all surpassing beings, like smoke in the breeze, the couple took the form of a man and a woman.

Suddenly a great bowl filled with water appeared nearby, and Earth Mother realized that each place in the world would be surrounded by mountains like the rim of the bowl. She spat in the water and, as foam formed, she said, "Look it is from my bosom that they will find sustenance."

She blew her warm breath over the foam, and some lifted, sending down mist and spray in great abundance. "So," she said, "just so will clouds form at the rim of the world where the great waters are and be born by the breath of the surpassing beings until your cold breath makes them shed downward—the waters of life falling downward into my lap where our children will nestle and thrive, finding warmth in spite of your coldness."

In this way, and many others, Earth Mother and Sky Father provided for their progeny, the people and the other creatures of the world.

Reworked by Jake Page and David Leeming

A Rig Veda Creation

Then even nothingness was not, nor existence.
There was no air then, nor the heavens beyond it.
What covered it? Where was it? In whose keeping?
Was there then cosmic water, in depth unfathomed?
Then there were neither death nor immortality,
nor was there then the torch of night and day.
The One breathed windlessly and self-sustaining.
There was that One then, and there was no other.
At first there was only darkness wrapped in darkness
All this was only unillumined water.
That One which came to be, enclosed in nothing,
arose at last, born of the power of heat.

In the beginning desire descended on it—
that was the primal seed, born of the mind.
The sages who have searched their hearts with wisdom
know that which is, is kin to that which is not.
And they have stretched their cord across the void,
and know what was above, and what below.
Seminal powers made fertile mighty forces.
Below was strength, and over it was impulse.
But, after all, who knows, and who can say
whence it all came, and how creation happened?
The gods themselves are later than creation,
so who knows truly whence it has arisen?
Whence all creation had its origin,
he, whether he fashioned it or whether he did not,
he, who surveys it all from highest heaven,
he knows—or maybe even he does not know.

Translated by A. L Basham

A Chuckchee Creation

In the beginning the great Trickster Raven, the self-created, lived with his wife in a tiny space. Bored with her existence, the wife asked Raven to create the earth. "But I can't," he said. "Well, then," said the wife, "I shall create at least something." She lay down to sleep, with Raven watching over her. As she slept, the wife seemed to lose her feathers, and then to grow very fat, and then without even waking up she released twins from her body. Like the mother, now, they had no feathers.

Raven was horrified, and when the twins noticed him they woke their mother and asked, "What's that?" She said, "It's father." The children laughed at the father because of his strange harsh voice and his feathers, but the mother told them to stop, and they did.

Raven felt he must create something since his wife had created humans so easily. First he flew to the Benevolent Ones—Dawn, Sunset, Evening, and the others—for advice, but they had none to give. So he flew on to where some strange beings sat. They were the seeds, they said, of the new people, but they needed an earth. Could Raven create one? Raven said he would try, and he and one of the man-seeds flew off together. As he flew Raven defecated and urinated, and his droppings became the mountains, valleys, rivers, oceans, and lakes. His excrement became the world we live in. The man-seed with him asked Raven what the people would eat, and Raven made plants and animals.

Eventually there were many men from the original seed, but there were no women until a little spider woman appeared and made women. The men did not understand about women, so Raven, with great pleasure, demonstrated copulation.

Leeming, *Creation*, 53–54

A Christian Creation

In the beginning was the Word, and the Word was with God, and the Word was God.

The same was in the beginning with God.

All things were made by him; and without him was not any thing made that was made.

In him was life; and the life was the light of men.

And the light shineth in the darkness; and the darkness comprehended it not.

There was a man sent from God, whose name was John.

The same came for a witness, to bear witness of the Light, that all men through him might believe.

He was not that Light, but was sent to bear witness of that Light.

That was the true Light, which lighteth every man that cometh into the world.

He was in the world, and the world knew him not.

He came unto his own, and his own received him not.

But as many as received him, to them gave he the power to become the sons of God, even to them that believe on his name:

Which were born, not of blood, nor of the will of the flesh, nor of the will of man, but of God.

And the Word was made flesh, and dwelt among us, (and we beheld his glory, the glory as of the only begotten of the Father,) full of grace and truth.

John, I: 1–14

An Icelandic Creation

The High One told Gangleri that once there were two places, one in the south that was all fire and light and one in the north that was icy and dark. The first was called Niflheim. The two atmospheres met in an emptiness between them called Ginnungagap. There the hot and the cold mixed and caused moisture to form and life to begin, first as the evil frost giant Ymir.

Ymir lay down in Ginnungagap and gave birth to a man and a woman from his armpits; one of his legs mated with the other to make a son. Thus began the family of frost ogres. Some of the melting ice became the cow giant, Auohumla, whose teats flowed with rivers of milk to feed the giant and his family.

As for the cow, she fed on the blocks of ice around her. As she licked the ice, a man gradually appeared from it. He was Buri the Strong; he had a son called Bor who married Bestla, a daughter of one of the frost ogres. Bor and Bestla produced the great god Odin and the gods Vili and Ve. These gods killed Ymir, and from the blood that resulted, all the frost ogres were destroyed in a flood. One giant, Bergelmir, escaped with his wife and family.

The three gods took Ymir's body to the center of Ginnungagap and turned his body into the earth and his blood into the seas. His bones became the mountains and his teeth and jaws became rocks, stones, and pebbles. The gods turned his skull into the sky, held up at each of the four corners by a dwarf. These are called by the names of the four directions. From Muspell they took sparks and embers and made the sun, moon, and stars, placing them over Ginnungagap.

The earth was made to be round and surrounded by the ocean. The gods gave shore lands to the descendants of the surviving giant family. They made a stronghold out of Ymir's eyebrows, and they made clouds of his brains. The three gods made man and woman out of two fallen trees, an ash and an elm. Odin breathed life into the new pair. Vili's gift to them was intelligence, and Ve's gifts were sight and hearing. The first man was names Ask; the first woman was Embla. The stronghold, Midgard, became their home, so they were protected from the cruel giants outside.

Sturluson, *The Prose Edda*, in Leeming, *Creation*, 134–35

A Modern Creation

The universe is a green dragon. Green because the whole universe is alive, an embryogenesis beginning with the cosmic egg of the primeval fireball and culminating in the present emergent reality. And a dragon, too, nothing less. Dragons are mystical, powerful, emerging out of mystery, fierce, benign, known to teach humans the deepest reaches of wisdom. And dragons are filled with fire. Though there are no dragons, we are dragon fire. We are the creative, scintillating, searing, healing flame of the awesome and enchanting universe.

Swimme, 171

COSMOGONY

The most essential and revealing of our collective dreams are our myths of how the universe and we were created—our cosmogonies. Cosmogonies are important perhaps for the same reason the exploration of the past and of origins has traditionally been important in psychoanalysis. The creation myth reminds us of who we are; it brings into the present time what Eliade calls the energies of the childhood of our cultural being, and it renews us. So it is that creation myths are typically recited during curing ceremonies. The Navajo shaman sings the creation myth as the patient sits at the center of the sacred world represented by the sand painting. Catholic and Anglican priests once read or chanted the first chapters of the Gospel of John, "In the beginning was the Word," at the end of Mass—the collective curing ceremony of Christianity. These rituals are logical, since curing means a chance to begin again, a chance for re-creation. A question now arises for late-twentieth- and early-twenty-first-century people. How does our scientific view of the world's creation energize our much more global society now, and how does a contemplation of that view bring us, through awe and wonder, to a curative state of re-creation?

The Greek roots and related roots of *cosmogony* are *genos/genea* (race, family, genealogy, genesis), *gonos* (offspring), *kosmos* (cosmos, universe). Thus, *cosmo-logia*, or *cosmology*, the study of the cosmos, and *kosmos + gonos*, or *cosmogony*. In our creation myths we tell the world, or at least ourselves, who we are. We describe our ancestry, our conception, our first home, our early relations with our progenitors, our place in the first world. In the process we reveal our real priorities, our real fears, our real aspirations, and sometimes our real prejudices and neuroses.

A CONFERENCE OF MYTH-MAKERS

If we could individualize and personify the collective cultural minds out of which the many cosmogonies of our world have emerged, and if we could place them together in one room, we would discover a collective attempt to make sense of who we are as a species, to make creation conscious of itself by way of an extraordinarily complex and imaginative set of metaphors. Each cultural representative would say, "To be sure, I wasn't there, but I can use types and places and aspects of my own experience of life and society to tell you what it must have been *like*." "This is who we are," says the Navajo (Dine). "We emerged at least four times from places below the present world." A chorus of Southwestern American myth-makers agree. "This is who *we* are," say the authors of the book of Genesis. "Yahweh created everything that is, including us, out of the void." The Christian scribe, his Muslim friend, and countless others from around the world nod in agreement. "Our world was created in a kind of dreaming," says the Australian aboriginal representative. "Someone dove into the primordial depths for our world," says the Iroquois, echoing something similar just announced by the writer of the *Viṣṇu Purāṇa* from India. And some Central Asian shamans whisper, "That happened for us, too." "Akongo created a perfect world that human dissension ruined," cries a Ngombe visionary. "Yes, and I'll bet he sent a great flood to punish humans," answer voices from all over the hall. The Ancient Egyptian myth-maker says, "We came from the secretions of the great god—from his spit and his hand-induced semen." "One of our first gods did that too," muses the representative of Vedism with some embarrassment. "We know about that, too," says the Boshongo storyteller. "Well, Raven shat and peed from the sky to create the mountains and the sea," mumbles a Chuckchee shaman, "and someone here just admitted that his god vomited the world." "Our ancestors separated Sky Father and Earth Mother so that we could have room to live," says the voice of the Maori. "That happened to us, too," says the Egyptian; "Geb and Nut had to be separated or we would have been suffocated." "Our ancient high god cut off his father's genitals to separate him from the first Mother," says a revived Hesiod. "And what about the fact that the earth itself is the result of an ancient dismemberment," argues a Mesopotamian with the enthusiastic support of various medicine people from Africa and North America. "As far as we are concerned mountains are the Mother's breasts, peninsulas are her fingers, the trees and the grass her hair." "But we originated in a great cosmic egg," interjects a Chinese sage. Representatives from Tahiti and many other places say they did, too. And so the conversation goes.

Already certain patterns are evident in the bits and pieces of the myths to which we have just alluded. Groups of compatible thinkers inevitably arrange themselves in our hall. A small group of *Deus faber* believers—those who compare the creation to some craft such as weaving or carpentry—gets together. A little knot forms of those who believe that creators fell from the sky. Smaller subgroups emerge as well. People from otherwise incompatible groups find common ground in seemingly isolated themes.

Ex Nihilo Cosmogonies

The largest group of our myth-makers has roots at least as early as the Neolithic civilizations of the Fertile Crescent. These are the believers in creation from nothing (ex nihilo) or from chaos or some sacred substance by a single Sky God, Supreme Being, or Father God.

This Supreme Being group includes representatives from ancient Egypt, Mesopotamia, and India, as well as the founders of Judaism and the Olympian Greek religion, and it also includes Christians and Muslims. In fact, it has representatives from most parts of the planet.

The group shares several dominant characteristics besides creation by the Sky Father. The creator is almost always male and all-powerful, and the world he creates is hierarchical. Humans—especially men—are the creator's representatives there. The Supreme Being mythmakers speak a great deal about special revelation. They tend to be argumentative and defensive. They ignore the likelihood that their mythic pattern displaced an older pattern in which a goddess figure representing fertility and agriculture was dominant. Particular *ex nihilo* peoples often see a special relationship between themselves and a personal God who reigns above as king of the universe.

Many of the Father God people—perhaps because of their commitment to the ideal of power—have, over the centuries, tended to insist on a literal rather than symbolical understanding of their myths. As a result, they are often at odds with each other and generally unwilling to see in the myths of others representations of their own beliefs. Although the one Yahweh/God/Allah of the three Abrahamic traditions is recognized as the same god by all three, Jews, Christians, and

Muslims have all—often in spite of scripture and earlier tradition—claimed exclusivity and have used that notion of exclusivity to justify the oppression of others, including each other. And even within the religions themselves scripture has often been distorted to support war against factions and sects or the oppression or even mutilation of designated segments of the species, including children, people of different skin color, and particularly women.

EARTH-CENTERED COSMOGONIES

Another, much smaller, group in our hall of creation myth-makers represents a significant alternative to the myth pattern of the distant Sky God. These are the emergers and animists—those who believe we were born of the Earth, of the eternal Mother, or that the Earth quite simply *is* the eternal living Mother. As was noted earlier, it seems likely that this group contains myths that existed before those of the Father God group. And despite the dominance of that group, the Mother people have held on to their beliefs in isolated areas such as the American Southwest, where small, often matrilineal societies still recognize the Mother creatrix as the most significant divine power even when distant Sun God creators are recognized as well. In several of the Southwestern cosmogonies the Sun is a kind, personal creative energy force that interacts with another original life force, the Earth itself, often identified with a figure known as Spider Woman or Thinking Woman. In this creation pattern the first people move into successive versions of existence until they finally emerge into this world by the *sipapu* or spider hole replicated in the kivas, or ceremonial chambers, of modern-day pueblos. Once people have emerged into this world, the arrangements of life are the responsibility of the Goddess or her female offspring.

CREATION BY EMANATION

There are mystics in the creation hall—Sufis and a few students of the Kabbala who had joined up earlier with various Hindus, Buddhists, and Christians to discuss their belief in creation by emanation from the mysterious essence of a nonpersonal Being—perhaps Brahman or En Sof, ultimate reality that is everywhere and nowhere. Brahman as referred to in the ancient *Atharva Veda* is the power within *mantras*. Later, in the *Upaniṣads*, Brahman is the ever-existing principle of creation itself. In the still later Vedānta philosophy of Hinduism, Brahman is the essence of everything that is. In the Kabbalistic understanding, En (or Ein) Sof is the transcendent God who is beyond the capacity of human thought, the essence from which all things emanate. Plato (c. 428–348 B.C.E.) joins this group, too, if perhaps a bit tentatively, with his idea of an eternal and constant reality from which humankind has become isolated but with which reunion is possible. This understanding is revealed in the well-known myth of the cave, in which our world is seen as merely a shadow of what Plato's follower Plotinus (205–270 C.E.) called the "One" from which existence emanates.

In the sixth book of the *Republic* Plato suggests that we imagine some men who have lived since childhood in a place underground that can only be reached by way of a tunnel-like passage that eventually opens to the light. Since the men are chained by the neck, they can only see what lies in front of them. Above and behind them is a fire that creates light and between them and the fire there is a track with a wall below it. The wall serves to hide people behind it much as puppeteers are hidden in a puppet show. These people move objects that appear on the track above them. The objects are representations of animals, inanimate figures, humans, and so forth. The prisoners cannot see the fire, the wall, or the track. They can only see the shadows on the wall in front of them caused by the objects and the firelight behind them. When the people behind the wall give voices to the models they move, the prisoners hear only the echoes of those voices. Plato says that the condition of the prisoners represents our own position in relation to the light outside the cave. Like us they are separated from the Source of Being and are doomed to see only shadows of Being until such time as they can achieve enlightenment.

A good example of creation by emanation is expressed by the Turkish faylasuf (mystical philosopher) Abu Nasr al-Fārābī (d. 980 C.E.). In what might be called his creation myth, Al-Fārābī followed Plato (and Aristiotle) by rejecting an ex nihilo onetime creation in favor of a chain of being emanating from the Logos, or Divine Reason, in ten successive intellects that take form as the Ptolemaic heavenly spheres. As far as our own world is concerned, there is a Platonic chain of existence extending from lower beings to the possibility of the human being reunited with Divine Reason itself.

In modern times theologian Paul Tillich (1868–1965) has viewed creation as an emanation from "ultimate concern" or "Ground of Being." Tillich would agree with Al-Fārābī that God as we have understood him is one of many symbols through which humans have attempted to communicate with a god who is beyond God, beyond understanding.

THE UNIVERSALISTS

A group of figures in the creation hall gradually form a larger new group that we might call universalist or planetary. Some members of this group are doing yoga, while others are studying the universe with their telescopes. Some have religious affiliation, some are atheists as far as any common understanding of God is concerned. Some are also members of the animist, emergence, and emanation groups already mentioned. Many are mystics. The universalists all agree that each cultural dream of creation represents a particular stage or aspect of a collective understanding. They realize that each creation story is absurd—obviously a "myth"—but also that each contains some revelation through symbol and metaphor, and that each, including one's own, necessarily represents only part of the truth.

The universalists remind us that, despite the restrictions of fundamentalism, as the human race has evolved, so has its understanding of creation. The understanding of creation, they say, has generally followed the conception of divinity (the subject of the next chapter). It is logical enough, therefore, that ancient agricultural societies envisioned a female Earth giving birth to life through fertilization by a male Sun. Later war-driven societies would just as logically have understood creation as the ex nihilo work of the given dominant divine warrior or Supreme Being while the Greek philosophers, Islamic faylusufs, and mystics of all traditions—people for whom divine power was ineffable and less personal—would have conceived of creation as emanating in stages from Being itself. Belief in an almost mechanistic so-called deistic or clockmaker creation coincided with the rise of science during the Enlightenment. Finally, the twentieth century produced a general belief among scientists, who have generally not included any particular God in the equation, that creation was the result of a huge explosion some twelve billion years ago in which space and time, along with matter, came spontaneously into being. This explosion, which filled the cosmos with the basis of life, a quark-gluon plasma, has now been mythologized as the "Big Bang" story, the details of which are still evolving.

For the universalist, each of these mythic patterns must be taken seriously; each represents a stage of our understanding of creation. If we can no longer accept the fundamentalist exclusivity of the Father God people, we, nevertheless, can appreciate, in light of our partial understanding of the Big Bang, the apparent accuracy of their ex nihilo idea of creation. From the Earth Mother people we can certainly accept the idea of the integral association of all aspects of life—including ourselves—as offspring of the same Earth, to whom followers of the James Lovelock–Lynn Margulis Gaia hypothesis have restored her ancient Greek name, Gaia. According to Margulis and Lovelock, the earth can be understood as a giant living organism, attending to its own needs—an organism of which we, for the moment, are interesting parts.

The universalist group in our creation hall, in fact, contains many scientists. Albert Einstein (1879–1955) is discussing with Werner Heisenberg (1901–1976) and Niels Bohr (1885–1962) questions of Relativity and Uncertainty. They agree that our very consciousness is crucial as an effect on any experiment. We were wrong to assume, following the Newtonian-Cartesian assumption, that given enough information we could know everything. Einstein is not so sure of that last point, however; he announces his intention of pursuing a Unified Field Theory that will eventually explain everything and resolve the contradictions of such theoretical constructions as Uncertainty and Quantum Mechanics. Nevertheless, Einstein's words contain the mystery of myth. Mass, he says—and that includes us and our physical world—is energy in relation to the speed of light, making matter and flesh something that can best be described as energy events. Furthermore, he tells us, time and space are in a sense physical realities (see Stannard, 10–12).

Maurice Merlau-Ponty (1908–1961) stands near the scientists in the hall and reacts with something like the old religious fervor to their extraordinary thoughts. He likes the idea of the flesh as energy event and suggests to theologian-philosopher Matthew Fox that the traditional denigration of the flesh as evil in the Abrahamic religions has dulled our natural wonder and awe in the presence of creation—the "flesh of the world." Fox enthusiastically agrees: "What is flesh?" he asks. "The clouds . . . the sun . . . the birds singing their morning cantatas . . . and we too. . . . Blessed flesh . . . Flesh is for joy, wonder, and delight" (Fox, *Sins*, 35). "We have always understood this," say animists from North America and Africa.

A NEW CREATION MYTH

The result of the failure of mainstream religion to keep up with the progress of human knowledge has been a general resistance or inability of ordinary people—those not on the radical fringes of theology and those out of touch with the esoteric disciplines of astro and microphysics—to experience, in the presence of current understandings, the emotional transcendence that would center us as the ancient stories of Genesis or the Earth Mother centered our ancestors. Even if we are intellectual admirers of Paul Tillich or the Islamic fay-lasufs, we might not find the actual experience of spiritual and/or emotional transcendence in their words. For most of us some projection of truth into myth is necessary—especially into art as story. "Tell me a story," says the child to the parent. "Explain it with a parable," says the follower of Jesus, Buddha, Bomba, or the Zen master. "Don't just tell me, show me."

Back in our creation hall, Catholic creationist theologian Thomas Berry and his follower Brian Swimme now suggest that what the universalists have gradually been doing for nearly a century is precisely compiling a new creation myth, one in which we humans play a much larger part than we did in the old myths. "That which created all of this," they say, "now desires *our* creativity, commitment and labor, *our* delight in entering with full awareness the cosmic story. . . . We are the creative, scintillating, searing, healing flame of the awesome and enchanting universe" (Swimme, 170–71). Without our consciousness, in other words, there is no creation in any meaningful sense. This concept will be elaborated later.

A mysterious new storyteller stands up in the hall and announces that he has had a vision of a new creation myth for his children, one based on our new understandings of the universe, but using traditional language patterns. His goal is to bring the universal and ethereal realm into that of the culturally familiar and in so doing to fulfill the universalist vision of humanity's role in creation.

"In the beginning was the Great Mystery," he begins. "Some have called the Great Mystery Logos or Brahman or God, but we call it the Great Mystery because no one knows what it was or is. *We* think that at the beginning it was full to bursting with potential energy—with the potential for everything that was, is, and will be—male and female, vegetable, mineral, and animal. This Energy became mass associated with the speed of light in a gigantic bursting of itself into the explosion that became the Universe. We can see the beginnings of the continually expanding horizons of the universe and in the distant stars. In the Milky Way, our own solar system, we can see later particles of the explosion. Our Mother Earth is one of these particles as she dances with other planets around the part of the Great Mystery that is the solar energy source. The Great Mystery as Mother Earth—call her Spider Woman or call her Gaia—is part of the continuing creative process: molding mountains and rivers, giving birth from her inner warmth and outer wetness to flecks of the Great Mystery, some of which, like plants, suck nourishment through roots from the Mother's inner body, some of which, like animals, like *us*, have learned to walk about seeking nourishment—Great Mystery Energy—from plants and from each other. The Mother has had to discard some of her children, but most she has kept and nourished. Among these tiny flecks of the Great Mystery explosion and its aftermath are we humans, who, like each cell in any given body, contain the information that is the whole body. The life that is in each of us is the life that is in the relatives who are the plants, the microbes, and the mountains—all traceable to the explosion of the Great Mystery. Like the parts of the body, we humans have a particular role to play in the larger body. Each group of us has a different metaphor for the Great Mystery and its embodiment in this world—Jesus, Buddha, Kṛṣṇa—and these are good metaphors. And we all have in us the aspect of the Great Mystery that we call consciousness. Other beings have it too, but in our case we have learned to conceive of beginnings, middles, and ends—of what some have called plot. We have learned to seek the whole picture, to tell the story of life, the story of the Great Mystery's creation that is itself the Great Mystery. In our paintings, our thoughts, our words, and our stories we have learned to imitate creation and make creation conscious of itself. As long as we keep doing this the Mother will not discard us. But if we turn only to our personal needs and stories or the selfish needs and stories of our own cultures or even our own species, we will dissolve like the great dying stars or the monster dinosaurs into oblivion."

Physicist Erwin Schrödinger (1887–1961) and several Islamic mystics, or Sufis, are greatly moved by the new myth. They speak of our being the sense organs of the world, of the world experiencing itself through our consciousness and our flesh. "Creation still goes on in us as we re-create in our consciousness. This is really what it means to have been 'made in the image of God.' If there is Eternity, we are already there," they say.

Most of the universalists agree that the old creation stories, like this new one, are spiritual parables or mantras, metaphors for the state of our knowledge at a given time and place. The stories were never meant to be taken literally; only in their symbolic guise do they speak to the scientific world as well as they once did to the pre-scientific world. As symbols they are powerful mantras; as literal stories they are merely fun or funny. Our universalists are planetary vision people; they speak of a mighty chorus of different voices in all parts of the planet, all celebrating symbolically the deep structure of the creation archetype, the chaos-to-cosmos pattern that in microcosm is the essence of all of our relationships, of every task we undertake. Indeed, re-creation, they say, is at the very center of our being. If we do not re-create, if we do not make creation conscious of itself, we have no reason for being.

Re-Creation as Recreation: The Role of the Arts

Nowhere is this human need to make creation conscious of itself more evident than in the strange human activity to which we apply the general term "art." There have always been those who have felt compelled to represent existence indirectly through art, even when such activities might well have been considered to be peripheral, time-wasting, or even treasonous. Remarkably, during the Paleolithic period, for instance, when humans were engaged in a desperate evolutionary struggle to survive, people took the time to paint—to re-create—in the caves.

"It's really all a question of science and the nature of reality," say the planetary visionaries. In fact, the natural tendency in any system, according to the Second Law of Thermodynamics, is the entropic pull toward disorder. Creation and re-creation struggle against that pull. It is the miracle of consciousness and creativity itself that define the human species and establish its essential relationship to the larger creation. In this sense, art is a metaphor for creation, an implicit celebration of consciousness and of the larger Creation. To study art is to study a reflection of the gradual development of an ongoing myth of creation.

The human need to tell the story of creation, the story of our relation to the universe, has been as present in our time as it was in the time of the Paleolithic cave painters or that of Homer and Hesiod, Michelangelo, and Tolstoy. These great artists all felt comfortable using the elements of traditional creation stories and traditional religious understandings of the universe as symbolic vehicles for their visions. As mainstream and especially fundamentalist institutions have gradually lagged further and further behind our scientific knowledge, however, the artists of the world, the painters, architects and writers—who have always been the ones to turn the views of theologians and philosophers into narrative and plastic forms accessible to the general populace—have had to find new symbols, new ways of celebrating whatever it is that gives us meaning, of celebrating the creation of which we are all a part.

CREATION AND MODERN ART

Several modern painters, musicians, and architects in the creation hall bring out their paintings, scores, and plans to show that they have been working in the same vein as the universalists. In fact, they point out, while the physicists were wrestling with the problems arising from the undermining of Newtonian and Cartesian absolutes at the turn of the twentieth century, they, as creators of art, were turning away from the kind of work based in these absolutes and were instead celebrating, in effect, the very consciousness that defines us as re-creators. In light of the development of the new science and the human need to tell a true story rather than merely to re-tell an old one, the emergence of modernism at approximately the same time as such theories as Relativity and Uncertainty is not surprising. The underlying characteristics of what we call modernism and postmodernism in the arts suggests that in the absence of valid symbols possessing numinous power, the artist turns for subject matter to the *process* of making art. We are made aware of this process as early as in the paintings of Van Gogh, which reveal through visible brush strokes and bits of bare canvas the struggle between the artist's vision and the resistance of the medium. We find it in the cubist painters, who consider from various perspectives the forms that make up the painting. We find it in the abstract expressionism of a painter such as Jackson Pollock, whose personal relation to his art emanated from paintings literally about painting. The same tendency is present in the early modernist eye-as-camera films of Vertov, in *cinema verité*, in the *nouvelle vague* cinema of Jean-Luc Godard and François Truffaut, as well as in recent films such as Liv Ulmann's *Faithless*. In a sense these are films about filmmaking, just as buildings like the Centre Pompidou or the Guggenheim Museum are buildings about building rather than metaphors, for instance, for Yahweh's Creation or Christ's body. Or modern artists take the old symbols and renew (traditionalists might say "distort") them so that they might speak to our new understanding. Salvador Dali's "Crucifixion" is more about space and its relation to geometry than it is about a particular religious event. The great cubist paintings of the early twentieth century eschew the linear logic of a renaissance perspective and conventional forms that reflect a particular kind of religious order in favor of a celebration of the dynamic makeup of those forms revealed simultaneously on the surface of the canvas. In this sense, the modernist work is a representation of the story of $E=mc^2$, or of Uncertainty, or of the simultaneous existence of light as particles and waves. The idea of the given work emanates directly from the "Ground of Being" that is the work itself, rather than from an intermediary symbol. To put it another way, if the relativity "myth" sees creation as a dynamic energy event, the cubist painting, for example, is that event in particularized microcosm. All of so-called "modern art" suggests the new scientific understanding that a perfect experiment is impossible because by performing an experiment we are, by our presence, affecting the outcome. In short, our consciousness must be seen as part of any equation. The art of the modernists and postmodernists represents the ongoing creation myth of which we are a functioning part. As will become clear later, this understanding of the role of consciousness will be important in the development of a new image of the hero.

VIRGINIA WOOLF'S <u>TO THE LIGHTHOUSE</u>

An example of a narrative work that epitomizes the modernist perspective on creation is Virginia Woolf's *To the Lighthouse*. In this novel, as in all modernist works of art, representational forms, if they are present at all, are distorted so as to force us to question our conventional ideas of reality and to become more acutely aware of the processes by which the artist creates and we perceive. What gives formal integrity to Woolf's work is the theme of creation itself. In fact, the novel is a metaphor for and even a conscious representation of the creative process.

Any modern creation story must, of course, be seen against the background of the creation pattern that emerges from our comparison of ancient creation myths. As we have seen, that pattern is one in which cosmos, or significant order, is formed in some way from chaos or original disorder. In many of the old myths humans are called upon to be the guardians and namers of creation and to struggle against evil forces within it, forces that would undermine order. Often the forces of evil win and the creator calls for a flood, a return to chaos, out of which a new creation can be born. The pattern has a modern analogue in the physics and mathematics that were being established in Woolf's time. Einstein's First Theory of Relativity, for instance, was published in 1905 and Heisenberg's Uncertainty Principle was established in 1927, the year of the publication of *To the Lighthouse*. In the world of the "New Science," dominated by the Second Law of Thermodynamics, energy is transformed from a random state into patterns of predictability. It has been suggested by the universalists in our hypothetical creation hall that it is the function of the human consciousness to de-code those patterns and thereby to give them interrelated significance in the face of an inevitable entropic pull toward a state of random equilibrium.

The underlying creation pattern or archetype and its thermodynamics analogue tell us that all creation is an unnatural defiance of the nothingness (literally nothing-ness) toward which the universe tends—an expensive one-time-only use of energy that can never be fully recovered again. The world of Adam and Eve, and of all nature, can be created, but the forces of disorder are immediately present in the "garden" seeking to regain dominance. Once the primal couple choose the way of knowledge of good and evil by eating the forbidden fruit, they can be redeemed, but only in the context of the ultimate payment, which is death—an entity that is a necessary part of the miraculous experience we call "life." What the Genesis creation myth and other creation myths do, when, through comparison, their archetypal pattern is revealed and they are seen in conjunction with the current understanding of creation, is to establish a model for the essence of human existence. The creation archetype tells us that only in the context of potential disorder can order become meaningful, that the fall from perfection, for example, because it imparts knowledge, or consciousness, and therefore makes every situation an opportunity for re-creation in a new medium, is a new opportunity for redeeming life from chaos. It is this fact that gives art its universal significance and urgency, for the artist's work can be seen as simply a model for the celebration of the essential human activity, without which we would be superfluous, the work that answers the eternal question, "What am I?"

As has been suggested, for the modern artist, revelation of this uniquely human role can best be achieved by the representation of the creative process. That is, the literal validity of the traditional and conventional systems having been challenged by science, modern art tends to be "scientifically" about itself. As Herbert Read has written, "It flies from discredited reality to create a 'new reality,' a realm of the absolute of mystical purity; and in so doing it makes use of the laws or elements that are fundamental to the structure of the physical universe" (28).

Significantly, then, *To the Lighthouse* is a novel about a woman's sense of arranging lives in order to stave off disaster, about a man who seeks determinacy against the strong force of indeterminacy, about a house that struggles against the leveling tendency of nature, and about a much-resisted completion of a voyage to a lighthouse. All of these plot elements can be seen as metaphors for essential elements of the thermodynamics order versus entropy view of creation. The novel is framed by the concept of creation itself, a framework provided by the painting of a portrait within which we find ourselves at the beginning of the novel, one that is only completed ten years later at the very moment when the central symbol, the lighthouse, is reached. The real tension of the novel is produced by the relationship between the artist Lily Briscoe's realization of her vision in the painting and the completion of the trip to the lighthouse. It is clear that Lily's "struggling against terrific odds" in her painting, her attempt to achieve order in chaos, is a metaphor for the analogous struggle of the novelist herself, and, by extension, of the human attempt through art to make creation conscious of itself. In an early version of her *Between the Acts*, Virginia Woolf commented on a modern dilemma: "We who have named other presences equally impalpable and called them God for instance or again the Holy Ghost, have no name but novelist or poet, or sculptor or musician for this greatest of all preservers and creators" (Richter, 138).

Lily's portrait of her friend Mrs. Ramsay and the latter's son James framed in a window at first looks back to older paintings based on the sacred image of the Madonna and child. This image, however, has lost its power to move the agnostic "modern" society of the novel and its creator and has therefore lost its power to hold off chaos. Art is always concerned with relationships among the various levels of our experience—conscious and unconscious, literal and figurative—and Lily Briscoe as the model of the modern artist must find a way of achieving a statement about those relationships as represented by the lives of the people around her. She must discover a pattern of significance, the realization of which individual illusions of separateness tend to work against, and she must do so not in terms of conventional representationalism and the symbolism of an earlier age but in terms of reality as understood in her own age—the age of the Big Bang, Relativity, and the Uncertainty Principle.

The problem facing Lily Briscoe, Virginia Woolf, and modern artists in general is how to depict reality when we "believe," for instance, that the structure of time-space, the world we live in, ultimately depends not on anything having to do with a literal Genesis but on the distribution of matter in the universe. For a painting to work, reality as we know it must be conveyed in microcosm in the closed system that is the canvas or the page, and for Lily Briscoe the mother and child achieve significance in terms of $E=mc^2$ rather than in terms of the Christian Virgin and child. In fact, the traditional story, as an easy solution to the technical problem facing her, might well become for Lily, as the modern artist, precisely an agent of the entropic drive toward noncommunication that must be overcome. There is nothing duller than the modern work that, however technically proficient, merely copies an older approach. The picture Lily is painting, she explains to a more traditionally minded companion, is "no attempt at likeness." Mrs. Ramsay and James are the dominant mass in a painting whose subject is the nature of reality as revealed in the "relations of masses, of light and shadows" (82). The objective must be to transfix momentarily the essential energy of life, to reveal by way of the creative source that is Mrs. Ramsay and James in the window the still point of cosmos in chaos, and in so doing to achieve the curative state of wonder and awe in the contemplation of creation.

Circumstances both personal and universal—death, including Mrs. Ramsay's, and war—intervene to put a stop to Lily's painting for some ten years. She returns to it, realizing that her brush is "the one dependable thing in a world of strife, ruin, chaos." She stands at her easel starting over again as the modern creator informed and given significance by the myth of the present time, the myth of consciousness striving against entropy. The blank canvas looks at her "with its uncompromising white stare. . . . One line placed on the canvas committed her to innumerable risks." The form enclosing "space" on the canvas "roused one to perpetual combat, challenged one to a fight in which one was bound to be worsted." Before she "exchanged the fluidity of life for the concentration of painting," Lily felt the "blasts of doubt," but she also felt the power of her vocation: "Her hand quivered with life, this rhythm was strong enough to bear her along with it on its current." But "the problem of space remained." The structure of space-time depends on the distribution of matter, and Lily's painting—her attempt at an answer to "what can it all mean?"—is this universal fact in microcosm: "The whole mass of the picture was poised upon that weight."

Lily's memories of the past—especially her vision of Mrs. Ramsay and James in the window—must be translated into the problem of representing space-time—the reality of creation. Where Raphael and the other great masters had begun with the divine myth, she must begin with the problem of the "significance of mother and son" as revealed in the relationship between lines and space. As the painting nears completion Lily seems to call out to the literal Mrs. Ramsay: " 'Mrs. Ramsay!' . . . the pain increased . . . no one had heard her cry that ignominious cry, stop pain, stop." This is the pain and cry of birth, the agony of the artist who must deliver a vision and a pain and cry archetypally analogous to the older "Why has thou forsaken me?" on the cross. Narrowly avoiding the "waters of annihilation," the painter returns to the "problem" before her—a representation in itself of the problem facing the conscious being: "The vision must be perpetually remade."

Meanwhile Lily looks out to sea and watches the widower Mr. Ramsay and the now teenage James as they reach the lighthouse in their little boat. At that moment, Lily's problems with space begin to be solved. As the space between her easel and the boat has become greater, it has also somehow become "full to the brim." Lily's realization, that of the modern artist, is similar to that of the modern scientist regarding the integral relationship between space or randomness—the "blank canvas"—and the "lingering" moments in which "life was most vivid." There can be no such thing as "empty" space when there are differentiated things. Everything that exists is a definition of space: "She seemed to be standing up to the lips in some substance, to move and float and sink in it."

The Uncertainty Principle tells us that it is impossible to know position and momentum of a moving particle at the same time. In Lily Briscoe's struggle, one can find the "phrases," the "visions," the "pictures," but not "the thing itself before it has been made anything." The lawn on which the artist's easel stands has become "the world," an Eden in which "everything this morning was happening for the first time." Lily is seeing her painting in the larger perspective of creation, and suddenly the vision of Mrs. Ramsay and James in the window returns, this time throwing "an odd-shaped triangular shadow." Once again Lily cries out, "Mrs. Ramsay!" and tries to keep the vision in her mind. In the triangle, itself, a symbol and building block of fundamental order, Lily finds a significant archetypal form for her modern version of the Virgin and child. Comparison will show us that Raphael and the other representational masters used the same archetype as the unifying force behind the structures of their versions of the subject. For Lily, that archetypal scaffolding, stripped of the details of the old myth, becomes itself the subject of her art. As Mr. Ramsay reaches the lighthouse, Lily imagines him standing heroically there "as if he were saying . . . 'There is no God'," and she finishes her now abstract painting by suddenly depicting Mr. Ramsay and his "heroism" by "drawing a line there, in the center of the triangle; It was done; it was finished. Yes, she thought, laying down her brush in extreme fatigue, I have had my vision" (238–310).

To the Lighthouse is the story of art's attempt as well as that of the human consciousness to participate in creation by achieving the still point at the core of reality. It is the story of the mother as creative artist and of the creative artist as mother. It is the story of re-creation in which the artist labors to give birth to the object that will place her subject in the larger context of human and universal significance. The archetype that had once taken form as the Virgin and child now conveys space defined by revelatory relationships between itself and line. Woolf takes the traditional story of the heroic quest and reconfigures it in the context of the new creation myth through which we can experience the awe and wonder of curative re-creation.

CHAPTER III

Deity

Myth and Gender

"Deity is the immanence and transcendence inserted in the heart of every being."

RAIMUNDO PANNIKAR

Eight Deity Myths

Ua Zit

Ua Zit was the world arising from a fiery island of the Nile, the womb that arose from the weeds of the delta, the Cobra Goddess who spread her hood so that the future would be known. Born again with each shedding of her skin, she was known as the Third Eye, the all-seeing eye in the holy forehead, and she spat forth her venomous and fiery spells of wisdom.

As Maat, the serpent eye, she was the cosmic order and rhythm, blind law, the wisdom traced in the veins of a leaf, the crystalline flint of a life's breath, the eye of morning and the eye of evening. She was balance, and the other deities delighted in her as food, for it was upon her nourishing wisdom that they feasted. On her head she wore a *maat*, the feather of an ostrich, and after one's death she would be found sitting on her heels on one side of the scales while the soul of the deceased was placed on the other. And if the scale was found to be in balance, the soul could depart victorious to mingle freely with the gods.

Ancient Egyptian Text,
reworked by Leeming and Page, *Goddess*, 45

Osiris and Isis

At his birth in Thebes a thunderous voice proclaimed the arrival of the Universal Lord. Osiris grew and was taller and more handsome than anyone. And he was gentle. Osiris loved his sister Isis, firstborn daughter of Geb and Nut. From one of Isis' tears the Nile had sprung. It is said that with the help of a serpent she tricked the ancient Sun God Ra into revealing the secret of his being.

Osiris and Isis became King and Queen and life never had been so good for the people or the land. But their younger brother, Seth, tricked Osiris into entering a beautiful coffer, sealed it shut and hurled it into the Nile, whose waters carried it out to sea.

Isis wandered the world looking for her beloved husband. She found his body trapped in a tamarisk tree in Byblos and brought it home. In Egypt she revived Osiris and in their passionate reunion Horus was conceived. But once again Seth encountered his brother and cut him into many pieces and threw him into the Nile. And once more it was the role of Isis to save her husband. She recovered the lost pieces, embalmed the body and sent Osiris off to be King in the Underworld. It is also true that Osiris, the God of Grain, was reborn as grain each year after the flooding of the Nile.

Leeming and Page, *God*, 83–86

Leda and the Swan [Zeus]

A sudden blow: the great wings beating still
Above the staggering girl, her thighs caressed

By the dark webs, her nape caught in his bill,
He holds her helpless breast upon his breast.

How can those terrified vague fingers pushed
The feathered glory from her loosening thighs?
And how can body, laid in that white rush,
But feel the strange heart beating where it lies?

A shudder in the loins engenders there
The broken wall, and the burning roof and tower
And Agamemnon dead.
      Being so caught up,
So mastered by the brute blood of the air,
Did she put on his knowledge with his power
Before the indifferent beak could let her drop?

W. B. Yeats

Yahweh

O clap your hands, all ye people; shout unto God with
    the voice of triumph.

For the Lord most high is terrible; he is a great King
    over all the earth. He shall subdue the people under
    us, and the nations under our feet.

He shall choose our inheritance for us, the excellency of
    Jacob whom he loved. Se'lah.

God is gone up with a shout, the Lord with the sound
    of a trumpet.

Sing praises to God, sing praises: sing praises unto our
    King, sing praises.

For God is the King of all the earth: sing ye praises with understanding.

God reigneth over the heathen: God sitteth upon the throne of his holiness.

The princes of the people are gathered together, even the people of the God of Abraham: for the shields of the earth belong unto God: he is greatly exalted.

Psalm 47

Sophia

Sophia, or Wisdom, is the female companion of Yahweh at the creation described in the Book of Proverbs. In the Gnostic tradition, Sophia was God's mother, the Great Virgin Mother in whom God was concealed before the beginning. For some Gnostics, Sophia was said to have been born of the female essence, Sige (Silence), and to have given birth herself to the male Christ and the female Achamoth. Achamoth produced Ildabaoth (Jehovah). When Ildabaoth denied humans access to the fruit of knowledge, Achamoth sent her own spirit as Ophis, the serpent, to teach humans to destroy Jehovah. The serpent was also seen as Christ. Later Sophia sent Christ to enter the man Jesus when he was baptized, and still later, Sophia and Jesus married in heaven.

Leeming, Creation, 256

Ala

In Ibo villages men and women join to build a small wooden house with a life-size image of the goddess Ala sitting on the front porch. As the people pass by they honor the Mother Goddess who is Earth. It is Ala who makes the seed in the womb grow into a child and she who gives the child life. It is she who remains with us during life and at death takes us back into her pocket.

Ala is always present. She gives the law, explains how those who live upon her may follow a life of righteousness and truth. She is always nearby—with child and sword—life and death.

Leeming and Page, *Goddess*, 38

Indra and the Ants

After Indra killed the universe-threatening demon, the gods all praised him as their savior, and in his glory he directed the architect of the gods in the building of a palace to end all palaces. But nothing the architect could do matched the god's vision of grandeur. In his despair, Indra appealed to Brahmā the Creator for help, and Brahmā appealed to the great god Viṣṇu, who agreed to help. [This he did in a very special way.]

A marvelously beautiful boy in pilgrim dress arrived at Indra's gate and asked to see the king. Indra greeted him and fed him honey, fruits, and milk.

Then the boy said, "I am told that you are building a palace to end all palaces; how long do you think it will take to complete? You realize, of course, that no other Indra has ever completed such a palace as you envision."

Indra was startled and amused that this mere boy, however wise he seemed, should presume to have known other Indras when there was surely only one Indra, King of the gods.

"How many Indras do you think came before me?" he asked with a wry smile.

"O King," the boy replied, "I have known all the Indras that have ever been and all the Brahmās, too. And I know the eternal Viṣṇu. I have watched the Indras come and go in an endless cycle of destruction and renewal—dissolving into the eternal darkness and being replaced through the power of Brahmā and Viṣṇu. You should know that there have been more Indras than grains of sand on earth or drops of rain from above."

Now a column of ants four yards wide began a parade through Indra's palace. The boy laughed and then was silent.

"Why are you laughing? Who are you?" Indra asked nervously.

"I am laughing because of the secret the ants are revealing—a great secret that destroys the proud."

"What secret? Please tell me," cried the god.

After the god pleaded more, the boy spoke with great authority. "Each of these ants," he said, "was once an Indra whose deeds made him King of the Gods. But each one, because of pride and wickedness, through many rebirths has become a mere ant. Just look at the poor army of one-time Indras crawling across your floor. Death is the master of all; even Brahmās come and go with each blink of Viṣṇu's eye. This world is only a dream."

after the *Brahmavāivarta Purāṇa*

The Tao

In the beginning was the Tao.
All things come from the Tao;
all things go back to the Tao.

Tao Te Ching

DIVINITY

The concept of divinity has apparently always been at the center of human consciousness and human life. We have indications of the concept at least as early as the cave paintings, rock carvings, and other artifacts of the Paleolithic period. Over time divinity has taken many forms and names. There have been sky gods, mother goddesses, fertility figures, tricksters, warrior gods. Figures such as Devī, Viṣṇu, and Śiva have dominated the temples and landscapes of India. Hera and Zeus ruled the heavens in Greece before they were displaced by the Christian God. Spider Woman and the

Great Mystery still exist in the sweat lodges, kivas, and mountains of North America. Nigerian Binis have their separated Mother Earth and Father Sky. The Japanese have their sun goddess Amaterasu, the ancestor of emperors. There are gods who become incarnated as humans—Christ, Lord Kṛṣṇa, and the other avatars of the great god Viṣṇu, and some would say the Buddha, not to mention the pharaohs of Egypt and the emperors of Rome and Japan.

There are, of course, many explanations for the concept of deity. A significant proportion of the human race argues that divinity first revealed itself to humanity in the form of personal beings such as those just mentioned, who have been or still are in direct communication with the world. This is the divinity type of many of today's organized religions, particularly those that worship the Abrahamic Yahweh-God-Allah. Others have seen deities as metaphorical expressions, symbols of the mysteries of the universe, reflections of our sense of the numinous, our sense of a realm of existence that is beyond the physical, beyond our understanding. For some, gods, being immortals, are the embodiment of our instinctive drive to establish a permanent order in the universe, of which we, as the allies or offspring of deities, can be a part if we act properly. For many, gods are as good an explanation as we have of where we and our world came from. In this light Mircea Eliade calls gods "fecundators" of the universe, embodiments of the mysterious force that, in creating, struggles against the natural tendency toward disintegration. If there is a universal theme reflected in the archetype that becomes our many versions of divinity, it would be our need to feel that we are meaningful inhabitants of a meaningful universe. In this sense, divinity is almost always fashioned in our image and is a metaphor for the furthest extension of which the human mind is capable at any given time. Deities, therefore, change with the times, taking ever new forms, even as the essential archetype remains constant, veiled in its eternal mystery.

THE EARTH GODDESS

It seems likely that our earliest sense of the numinous would have been expressed in a female metaphor reflecting the rhythms of nature. Women give birth and so does Earth. So Earth logically became Mother and then Mother Goddess. Paleolithic evidence articulated by Marija Gimbutas, Anne Baring, Jules Cashford, and many others gives strong support to this scenario and to the importance and perhaps even dominance of this early female deity. The ancient peoples of Anatolia, for instance, clearly worshiped a large birthing Mother Goddess as indicated by artifacts and excavations in places such as Hacilar and Çatal Hüyük (c. 6000 B.C.E.). Deities tend to reflect the political and social realities of those who depict them. Whether or not a dominant goddess in several forms presided over Paleolithic and early Neolithic matriarchies is unclear. We do know that the original great Goddess's descendants play a significant role in a deity biography of sorts that involves the rise of the male god to prominence at her expense and that parallels the movement from a female-centered agricultural society to a male-based warrior society.

Mythic evidence of the ancient Great Mother is scarce, due primarily to the nonexistence of writing. There are indications, however, in the Bronze Age cuneiform script of the Sumerians of a still powerful goddess who has retained much of the power of the hypothetical earlier figure. This goddess, Inanna (later Ishtar), descends to the underworld to confront the ravages of death in the form of her sister. It is she who performs the ritual love act on which the earth's annual rebirth depends. "Who will plow my high field?" she sings. "Who will plow my wet ground?" It is her shepherd-king-lover Dumuzi-Tammuz who provides this service, the seed bearer who "molded me with his fine hands . . . irrigated my womb" (Leeming, *Goddess*, 19, 60). This fragmented myth suggests that Dumuzi is a sacrificial king, one who must die for the good of all, the seed that must be planted. As such he is the ancestor of the Egyptian Osiris and the Christian Jesus, to mention only two of many Dying Gods. In the Dumuzi myth Innana has already entered the process in which the goddess will lose power to the god. Like the great Isis in Egypt and Cybele in Anatolia, she is a transitional figure who has moved from dominance to a position in which she has become primarily a fertility goddess dependent on the male seed.

Other remnants of the ancient Mother can be found in various societies that retain certain Neolithic lifestyle characteristics or have given them up only relatively recently. The Okanaga people of Washington State think of the Earth animistically as the "Old One," a female figure whose flesh is the soil, whose hair is plant life, whose bones are rocks, and whose breath is the wind. We live on and take sustenance from her body. And we are at her mercy. When she moves, for instance, there is an earthquake. A similar belief surrounds the goddess Kunapipi among the aboriginal people of Arnhemland in Australia. The pre-Aryan Indus Valley culture seems likely to have been presided over by a strong goddess whose descendant is the still powerful Hindu Devī (Goddess) who, nevertheless, is in some sense now subservient to her husband, usually the god Śiva. Devī wears many masks: Mā, the eternal Mother; Durgā, the terrifying monster-slayer; Pārvatī, the clever but nurturing daughter of the Himalayas, wife of the yogic Śiva; and Kālī, whose bloody fangs and death-dance celebrate the necessary cycles of life, the eternal destruction and reconstruction—the breathing of the universe. Kālī's black skin, like the skin of the later Black Madonnas of Italy, Mexico, Poland, and France (Chartres), is the dark fertile soil, the flesh of Earth herself. The Yuruba Oya is another such figure— she of the "insatiable vagina, the purifying wind"—as is the frightening Polynesian volcano goddess Pele.

THE SKY GOD

The role of the goddess deteriorates with the invasions of so-called Indo-Europeans or Aryans into the Near and Middle East, the Indian subcontinent, and Europe during the Bronze Age (c. 3500–1000 BCE). These invaders were warriors whose primary deities were almost certainly war gods associated with the sky rather than the earth, with conquest rather than nurturing, with light rather than mystery, and with stern father-hood rather than loving motherhood. The ancient pre-Aryan goddesses had taken their power from the earth rather than from the heavens. With the emergence of cities, the domestication of animals, and the develop-ment of the technology of war, male power took prece-dence over female birth-giving mystery. Mystery cults, of course, continued down through the centuries and fertility rituals were important, as indicated by the con-tinuing myths of Ishtar, Isis, Cyble, and others, but fer-tility goddesses increasingly came under the control of male gods. Demeter and Persephone in Greece were strong, but when Persephone was abducted by the underworld god Hades and Demeter removed her blessing from the land, causing it to wither, it was the all-powerful father Zeus who mediated the argument. And in the compromise he arranged, Hades was able to retain his victim as his wife even though she was allowed to return to her mother for half of each year.

In some cases the goddess, clearly reflecting a pervasive male view, becomes the nagging wife who restricts her husband's freedom. The famous Zeus–Hera relationship reflects this syndrome, as do aspects of the Śiva–Pārvatī relationship in India. In many cases the Great Goddess seems to fade away altogether, as in the case of the Celtic Mother Goddess Danu or the Greek Great Mother Gaia about whom we hear only fragmented stories. In still other cases goddesses are masculinized or turned into dangerous seducers whose sexuality undermines male power. The well-armed Athena is an example of the former, as is the virgin huntress Artemis, who in an earlier incarnation in Asia Minor had been the fertility goddess of many breasts. Aphrodite is an example of the latter. In the Babylonian epic of Gilgamesh, the male–female struggle and the superiority of the male are signaled when Gilgamesh refuses the sexual advances of the goddess Inanna/Ishtar, not wishing to fall into the trap that destroys later heroes such as the shorn and thus emasculated

Samson of the Bible. Similar scenes are popular in Indo-European myth. The Celtic Cuchulainn, for example, refuses the advances of and offers of help from the goddess Morrigan, claiming that as a male warrior he has no need of a woman's assistance—even that of a goddess. There is a clear belief in many of the post-Aryan invasion stories that the presence of women and of sexuality can only undermine the strength and dominance of men. The Athabascan peoples of North America tell the tale of the Vagina Girls, walking vaginas lined with teeth that devour men. It takes a great hero or man-god to tame these beings for proper male use by detoothing them. In all of these myths the female is dangerous because she is desirable. Therefore, the body is dangerous, something to be despised ("the flesh is weak"), and in religious traditions the intangible soul becomes an all-important counterweight.

Myths such as those of Pandora, who, because of the female "weakness" of curiosity, releases all manner of evil into the world from her box, and Eve, who leads Adam astray with the forbidden fruit, are archetypal relatives of seducers like Ishtar and Morrigan, even though their names clearly suggest earlier, more positive functions. Eve's name connotes motherhood. In a Mesopotamian form, corroborated by the Indo-European etymology of Ieva-Devi-Mā, she is a creatrix, the Mother of All Life and the consort of the serpent, himself a version of that ancient god, the often ithyphallic Trickster, who changes shapes at will and is at least in part a metaphor for natural human appetites necessary for life. The Trickster has many embodiments: the clever Hermes in Greece; the Spider Ananse in Africa; and Coyote and Raven in North America are just a few. As the serpent, he is often the consort-companion of female deities, such as the Great Goddess of second-millennium Crete, who was often depicted holding snakes aloft, and the Aztec Mother Coatlicue, who was adorned with the heads of serpents.

Under the new gods, women became objects of conquest and reproductive and sexual vehicles to be owned. The cult of virginity emerged as a means of ensuring individual male ownership. Important objectives of war were the "ravishing" of city walls and of the maidens within. In ancient Sumer rape had been punishable by death; later Semitic Indo-Europeans in the Fertile Crescent executed married women who were raped. The old, once sacred mysteries of womanhood were mythologically transformed into negative entities like Harpies, Sirens, and witches.

The second-millennium Babylonian creation story, the Enuma Elish, is a landmark in the deterioration of goddess power. In the myth we are told that in the land where Inanna had once reigned, the god Marduk became dominant, coming fully to power precisely by defeating and destroying the primeval mother of the waters, now a dangerous and mysterious monster with a horrid, venom-filled brood. So too was the goddess Gaṅgā subdued by Śiva in India and the dragon-serpent Python by Apollo, the god of light in Greece. The Sky God, now free of the Earth Goddess, was able to create the world, often ex nihilo, in his role as King of the Universe. Eventually he took form among the Semites of the Middle East as Abraham's tribal god, as Yahweh (YHWH = the unpronounced tetragrammaton signifying the Lord—"Adonai"), and later as God and Allah (al-Lah = the god), a deity who had no female consort.

THE FALL OF THE GODDESS: A SELF-EXAMINATION

This lack of a consort gives rise to many questions. A generally accepted truth of psychology, the source of one of the dominant myth systems of the modern era, is that we are what and who we are not only because of our genes but because of our "background" experience, an important part of which is our parenting. Creation myths are collective stories of parenting. In these myths our worlds, our cultures, and we ourselves were created by the original parents, our deities. When we are asked about these parents, there will inevitably be limitations on our actual knowledge but also, as the myths of psychology teach us, on what we are able to "face." And, of

course, our parents—actual and cosmic—are themselves the products of a past. The study of deities, like
the memory and evaluation of parents, involves a complex process of delving into the past and overcoming
strong forces of what contemporary psychology would
call "denial." It often means seeing our parents' limitations and the inadequacies of our visions of them.

A way to understand the power of the Abrahamic
God is to consider him in the context of the biblical
creation myths as illuminated by psychology. An
important element in the quest for the truth about ourselves is the need to break out of the shell of exclusivity
by moving from self-centered understandings to a more
comparative or general symbolic level of understanding. Our own fathers become more understandable
when compared to other fathers, and our relationships
with our mothers become more understandable when
compared to the behavior of other mothers and their
children. In the same way, deities and our relation to
them become more understandable when we move
beyond the parochial to the universal. To confront the
deities of the world is to begin a collective act of self-
examination.

To help us begin this self-examination, we might
assume a collective patient, a personification of so-
called Western culture itself, one purposely exaggerated
for purposes of emphasis. Our patient is referred to as
"he," only because our culture has traditionally been

patriarchal. In this case we must, of course, play both the role of analyst and that of patient. Our client enters our collective consulting room and lies down on the inevitable mythic couch, and we begin, according to the traditional view, at least, at the beginning, at the potential source of our problems. The assumption here at the center of the psychological myth is similar to that of the archetypal hero's descent into the underworld—a theme to be considered more fully later in this study—that to be whole we must first rule the inner world. If we can recognize the source of our problems in our inner worlds, we will have taken a major step toward self-realization. In the case of our particular collective patient, these problems are many and complex. There are unhealthy fixations and prejudices, aggressive tendencies, a debilitating lack of self-esteem, and irrational delusions, to mention only a few.

"Tell me about your childhood," we begin. "Where do you come from, and who were your parents? Tell me your God myth as you remember it."

OUR FATHER

"Well," our patient answers, "Our *Father* who art in Heaven exists eternally and he created the Universe in seven days. He created Angels of various ranks and under them He created Adam and Eve out of dust or, some say, He created Eve out of Adam's rib. In any case, He created a world full of creatures for these first humans and told them to procreate, to take dominion over creation and to name everything. Eve in her weakness fell prey to a jealous angel, who, in rebellion against God, disguised himself as a serpent and persuaded her to eat some of the forbidden fruit of the Tree of Knowledge of Good and Evil in the Garden of Eden, where Adam and Eve lived. And then Eve—like all women, always self-doubting, needing companionship, driven by guile—convinced Adam to eat, too, and the apple stuck in his throat (that's how we got Adam's apples). The couple now knew about good and evil and they became very sexually active and guilty about their desires. They found that covering themselves with leaves—especially fig leaves—only added to the lascivious feelings that haunted them. Anyway, although they tried to hide from our creator Father, they were found out, expelled from the garden, and made to work and to die. Women ever after were condemned to be afraid of snakes and subservient to men. There's a lot more: serious sibling rivalry and a sibling murder; a general wickedness, resulting in a punishing flood and the establishment of a chosen race called Hebrews or Jews, who were later followed by offshoots called Christians and Muslims. All three of these groups tend to think they have a special path to God—Allah and Yahweh really mean God—but, given my internal struggles and divisions, you would never know that. Well, that's about all I know about my family's early days."

This is clearly a simplistic understanding of Genesis in the intellectual sense, but it is essentially the version of the myth that exists in the collective Judeo-Christian psyche.

DENIAL OF THE MOTHER

As the collective analyst, we are, of course, faced with many obvious questions or points of discussion here. We could begin, for instance, with God.

"How do you feel about him? Do you feel comfortable talking about him as a Father? Are you afraid of him? Was Freud right when he suggested that 'god is in every case modeled after the father and our personal relation to god is dependent upon our relation to our physical father, fluctuating and changing with him, and god at bottom is nothing but an exalted father?' (Freud, 190). If God brought you up to be curious about things, should he have punished you for eating the fruit? And if you were commanded to procreate, could you have done so without the mysterious desires that followed the sin in the Garden? And, by the way, you speak of God the Father, but what of God the Mother? Experience teaches us that for any serious creation of life we need both. Why have you left out the mother?"

Of course it is true that most liberal-minded theologians and other religious people would agree intellectually that God, if immortal, is out of the procreative cycle and, therefore, genderless. But in the collective psyche, fed by scriptural and liturgical language, artistic depiction, traditional myths, and commonly attributed characteristics—especially of fatherhood—God—certainly in the Abrahamic tradition—is male.

It is a generally accepted fact of psychology that a lack of parental attachment—especially attachment to the mother or arbitrary treatment by the father—can lead to serious behavior problems in children. Could our cultural behavioral problems, such as our dependance on hierarchy and dominance, our alienation from the environment, our distorted gender roles—problems elaborated in the next section—have anything to do with our aloof and arbitrary father and missing mother?

The questions addressed to our fictional patient are perhaps those of psychological myth, but they are pertinent because the events that lead to them suggest a particular understanding of life and of creation. The most obvious human metaphor for creation comes from the female act of giving birth, as, for instance, in the creation myths that use the emergence metaphor, in which the people enter the world from the earth-womb. Yet our creation is male-dominated and the female aspect at the level of deity has been essentially eliminated.

This male-dominated view of the origins of the

universe is not limited to the Abrahamic religions but is predominant in all of the patriarchal Indo-European warrior cultures previously discussed. In the myths of these religions we find reflections of a likely culture struggle between an agricultural-based mother goddess society and a war-based warrior god society—the former being dominated by figures such as the huge fertile goddesses of Hacilar and Çatal Hüyük, the latter being represented by Indra-Zeus-Atum-Marduk-Yahweh. In the Homeric Hymn to Earth we hear that Gaia, or Earth, was the source of all things, "the Mother of us all." Hesiod supports the Gaia theory, claiming that the "wide-bosomed Earth" sprang from Chaos, but he notes that she was covered by her self-generated offspring Uranos, resulting in the birth of Kronos, or Time. Kronos hated his father for covering his mother, who complained to her son about the father's brutality, and he proceeded to separate his parents by inserting his cycle between them and castrating the father. He then went on to rape his sister Rhae—a deity who looked and acted very much like his mother and also was associated with Earth—and she gave birth to Zeus and the other Olympians—philandering, raping, frighteningly arbitrary males, whose sisters, wives, and daughters tended to be either masculinized huntresses and warriors like Artemis and Athena, or nagging high-maintenance wives like Hera, or fawning vamps like Aphrodite. Even some

important births the patriarch Zeus took care of himself; Athena was born of his head and Dionysos of his
thigh. The mythology of Greece is second only to the
Bible as a provider of metaphors for deity in the collective Western psyche.

THE FATHER GOD AND US

It seems fair to say that the belief in male power and
the right of the male, because of that physical power,
to dominate society is at the center of much of the
world's social being. It is reflected in monumental
architecture, the celebration of conquest in its many
forms, and in nationalism itself. It can be argued that
the dominance of the Father God myth has led to a
general acceptance of the human dominion over
Nature and particular territory in God's name as well
as to the separation of morality and religion from
responsibilities for the environment. Male power is
also reflected in the concept of judgment and retribu-
tion, in the importance our society attributes to hierarchy, as well as in the universally accepted idea in both
education and business, for instance, of proving oneself
by advancing over others. In American society it has
been common to justify many of these characteristics
through what might be called the "myth" of the
Protestant work ethic.

Furthermore, a religious-based belief in the cult of male reason and order as a natural adjunct of male power has resulted in the suppression of feminine values, of nonphysical power, and of women in general. The myth of female disorder and lack of reasoning power has been prevalent at least since the second millennium BCE, in myths such as that of the Mesopotamian Marduk's defeat of the female primeval power, Tiamat. Later mythic examples of the disruptive female are the Greek goddesses Hera and Aphrodite and the Celtic Meave. The effects of this negative vision of the female have long been evident in marriage, education, the workplace, and in religious hierarchy. Although many religious groups have made great strides in this area, the female question is still an issue in most religious traditions. Theology, scripture, and custom are still used to justify the subservient status of women, who are often associated with a negative view of sexuality. Finally, the relegation of sexuality to the lower spheres of existence as something dangerous and essentially evil—even if "God-given" and necessary to survival—is a pervasive product of the male-dominated mythology.

To stimulate the memory of our collective patient, to help him dredge up the repressed Mother—the lost Goddess—as a balance to the dominant Father, it will be useful to suggest some mythological figures and stories as questions for thought.

THE WOMEN IN GOD'S LIFE

Did the Abrahamic God ever have a wife? Did he divorce her? We know that one tradition holds that Adam, God's first human creation, had a wife before Eve and that she was called Lilith. Apparently she was too arrogant to lie in the passive position under Adam and chose to leave her husband when he demanded that she do so, thereby becoming the first feminist rebel. Some say Yahweh too had a wife, Asherah, the great goddess of Ugaritic Canaan who was worshiped in sacred groves representing her fruitful, life-creating loins. In popular Hebrew culture she was sometimes called the "Queen of Heaven," a position denied by the religious hierarchy who railed against Asherah worship.

From early on Christians longed for a mother, a feminine addition to the lofty, if now loving, male Trinity. They found one in Mary. In scripture the early church had made Mary a symbol of proper obedience—perhaps feminine obedience. "Be it unto me according to thy word" is one of the few statements attributed to her in the New Testament. But throughout the Middle Ages and Renaissance and down to our own age, the people, in effect, have demanded the recognition of Mary as an incarnation of the Great Goddess. To a great extent this demand was made possible by the scriptural claim of Jesus's virgin birth, a miracle built on in later traditions of Mary's own immaculate conception, dormition (sleep rather than death), and bodily assumption into heaven. Yet, ironically, it was the virginity, the denial of sexuality, the Immaculate Conception and the Assumption (both doctrines only accepted officially by the Roman Catholic Church in the mid-nineteenth and mid-twentieth centuries, respectively), that, as Jung reminds us (*Job*, 77), deprived Mary of much of the earthiness and the sexuality usually associated with the Mother Goddess. Still, Mary retains something of the earth-based aspect of the archetype. She appears unexpectedly to the downtrodden and lowly as the Virgin of Guadalupe or of Lourdes, and she acts as a direct intermediary to God. Despite official Church doctrine to the contrary, Mary, celebrated in countless works of art and especially in the thousands of great churches dedicated to her, is at the very least, as Anne Baring and Jules Cashford suggest, a goddess in the making (549ff). Joseph Campbell reminds us that it was in Ephesus, a center for ancient Great Goddess cults, that in 431 Mary was named Theotokos, or "God bearer": "And so it came to pass that Mary, Queen of Martyrs, became the sole inheritor of all the names and forms . . . of the goddess-mother in the Western world: Seat of Wisdom . . . House of Gold . . . Refuge of Sinners . . . Queen of Angels . . . Queen of Peace" and Queen of Heaven (*Masks*, 3:44–45, quoted from the fifteenth century "Aspirations from the Litany of Loreto").

The Survival of the Mother: The Great Emergence

At this point our collective patient might turn in his search for the lost mother to remnants of the old Neolithic Mother Goddess myths such as the female-centered emergence creation myths of the American Southwest. The emergence creation myths, as we have seen, eschew the dominant, male-based ex nihilo creation in favor of the more compatible metaphorical relationship between birth and creation.

The Pueblo people of the Rio Grande, the Hopi, and the Navajo all have versions of the great emergence. In some cases there is a male figure somewhere in the beginning, but he fades in significance with the arrival of a Mother who is more often than not Spider Woman, she who spins the universe into existence and sometimes creates two sisters who work out the details of the creation. In a sense it is from the Earth womb—the womb of the Goddess—that the people emerge in several stages from worlds below this world. Each emergence is a birth into a new state, and perhaps there will be later emergences. This creation myth is reflected in ritual dances and in the feminine architecture of the modest, earth-hugging hogan or the usually circular kiva, with its symbolic birth entrance or *sipapu* in the center of the floor and its equally symbolic smoke hole in the roof out of which the dancers emerge from the otherworldly darkness into the dance plaza of this world.

LESLIE MARMON SILKO'S <u>CEREMONY</u>

In this novel by a Laguna Indian woman, the emergence myth stands as a model for the positive revival of what might be called goddess power in our Father God-centered world. The novel tells the story of the redemption of a spiritually broken and alcoholic man who is the child of two cultures—one centered in the feminine life force, one sadly dominated by a kind of mechanistic sexist death force masked by concepts like progress and heroism.

"Ceremony" is a word that can suggest the human necessity to tell stories, to make creation conscious of itself through myth and ritual—to react to life mimetically and in so doing to stave off the undifferentiating entropy discussed earlier.

In the mythical conversation between a He and a She at the beginning of Silko's book we read these words:

I will tell you something about stories,
   [he said]
   They aren't just entertainment.
   Don't be fooled.

They are all we have, you see,
    all we have to fight off
    illness and death.

You don't have anything
    if you don't have the stories

    —

And in the belly of this story
the rituals and the ceremony
    are still growing.

    [What she said]
 The only cure
 I know
 is a good ceremony,
 that's what she said.

The novel itself, like any good ceremony, has a beginning, a middle, and an end—a true *mythos* or Aristotelian "plot." The plot reflects the process of creation itself, from Chaos to Cosmos—from nondifferentiation or non-self-realization, to struggle (*agon*), to differentiation or self-realization.

Tayo, our hero—our representative—is a conflicted being, plagued in this fifth world of emergence by the two forces reflecting his conception—whiteness and Indianness. The first—the world of his Anglo father—calls, on the one hand, for individual salvation through

Jesus Christ and on the other for the sloughing off of the superstition of Indian ways in favor of reason, nationalism, justifiable war, and progress. The world of his Indian mother calls for a return to the earth, the Mother, and the possibility of healthy survival only in the bosom of the community—the kiva with its ceremonies. Tayo is impressed by the white ways—the clothes, the cities—and he drifts away from the People—first as a soldier who kills in the white man's war and then as a psychopath and a drunk broken by the betrayal of his innermost being. This is the beginning. The middle is the main part of the ceremony: the quest for the cure. There are those who believe the old ways—a cure in the kiva by the medicine man—will be enough. But the world is different now. In Tayo's blood and in the world of the Laguna are the demands of two worlds. The old ways, the old myths, can only go so far. The Laguna medicine man who tries to help remembers even in the old stories the way the people turned against themselves and their creation. The world is a fragile place he tells Tayo. We humans have a purpose here. When the human being loses his harmony with the world, terrible things can happen and strong cures are needed. This theme is developed when Tayo is sent for the next stage of his cure—his ceremony—to experience the strong medicine of the shaman of another tribe, the old Navajo Betoni. Betoni shares with his patient a mixed heritage and understands that in this new fifth world of the emergence a new kind of curing is necessary. He performs the sand painting ceremony of the Navajo, which is now only a stage in the larger curing process. He directs his patient to something stronger and more mysterious—something new but strangely old and original. What Tayo—and, by extension, *we*—lack is the feminine life force to overcome the mechanistic death force. His achievement of self-hood is only realized by merging with the ghostly *anima* that is the mysterious Montaño Woman. With the Montaño Woman sexuality is curative. Through her Tayo learns that his flesh is indistinguishable from the flesh of the world. He learns to love himself as part of the earth of which his community is the living ceremony. The end of the story—or this part of it—is Tayo's successful overcoming of the temptations embodied in his former Indian friends who are destroyed by the witchcraft of the mechanistic death force. Tayo returns to his community, sure now of his identity and the source of his being:

> He stepped high over the steel rails and went down the cinder-bank roadbed toward the river. When he felt the dampness of the river, he started running. The sun was pushing against the gray horizon hills, sending yellow light across the clouds, and the yellow river sand was speckled with the broken shadows of tamaric and river wil-

low. The transition was completed. In the west and in the south too, the clouds with round heavy bellies had gathered for the dawn. It was not necessary, but it was right, and even if the sky had been cloudless the end was the same. The ear for the story and the eye for the pattern were [the people's]; the feeling was theirs; we came out of this land and we are hers.

In the distance he could hear the big diesel trucks rumbling down Highway 66 past Laguna. The leaves of the big cottonwood tree had turned pale yellow; the first sunlight caught the tips of the leaves at the top of the old tree and made them bright gold. They had always been loved. He thought of her then; she had always loved him, she had never left him; she had always been there. (Silko, 255)

Suddenly our planetary-universalists from the creation hall come into our consulting room. They have heard us talking about Tayo and the Montaño Woman and they are nodding their approval. "This is what our new story—our emerging myth—is all about," they say. Wallace Stevens is among them. "Have you read my 'Idea of Order at Key West'?" he asks. "There's a mysterious female singer there who will certainly make you think of the Montaño Woman and flesh and what our friend Matthew Fox here would call the 'Blessings of the Flesh'."

It was her voice that made
The sky acutest at its vanishing.
She measured to the hour its solitude.
She was the single artificer of the world
In which she sang. And when she sang, the sea,
Whatever self it had, became the self
That was her song, for she was the maker. Then we,
As we beheld her striding there alone,
Knew that there never was a world for her
Except the one she sang and, singing, made.
(from Stevens, "The Idea of Order at Key West," 54)

THE NEW MYTH OF DEITY
AND A BIOGRAPHY

The new myth can be contained even in the symbolic and universal language of the old myths and rituals of Brahman, Jesus, the Buddha, and Spider Woman—if that language is freed from narrow exclusivity and fundamentalism. The Catholic Thomas Berry can speak of a cosmic Christ, and the Islamic Sufi philosopher Muid ad-Din ibn al-Arabi (1165–1240) of the creation of God by the imagination in the inner self. The new myth tells the story of the endless development of Cosmos out of Chaos and of the interrelatedness of all things—atoms, mountains, people, woods, rivers, and microbes—in a fragile community of which it is urgent that we become aware not only as romantic or objective observers, but as outgrowths of Gaia with at least a temporary mission of consciousness.

That consciousness, itself represented by the dream of deity, continues to reach out for more knowledge, as the Jesuit paleontologist Pierre Teilhard de Chardin (1881–1955) and others have suggested. It is not enough to substitute the feminine for the masculine in our mythology any more than the masculinization of the feminine in education and business is a proper goal for society. Rather, we must listen to our universalist myth-makers, who have always searched for new expressions of deity, new means of articulating who we are in relation to the universe. Each civilization must develop its own symbolic structure. As Heinrich Zimmer once said, "We cannot borrow God. We must effect His new incarnation from within ourselves" (quoted in Campbell, *Masks*, 4, 626).

There are many new expressions of deity, some of which have already been mentioned in the preceding chapters. Karen Armstrong in her *History of God* traces the Western version of the archetype from its earliest stages through the establishment of the monotheistic religions, to the remote intellectual god concepts of the philosophers, to the universal inner god of the mystics, which is so important to the later universalists. It is the mystic's God of whom the German Meister Eckhart (c. 1260–c.1327) could write, "God gives birth to the Son as you, as me, as each one of us . . . as many gods in

God." Such a God is beyond male and female, as is the Brahman of the Vedic Upaniṣads, the impersonal Absolute that informs everything that is. The Jewish Kabbalists have a similar concept of a non-gendered God in En Sof ("Endless"). And the God of the Islamic Sufis is not much different. Celaladin Rumi provides what is perhaps the clearest vision of the mystic's God when he writes:

> Ground yourself, strip yourself down
> To blind loving silence.
> Stay there, until you see
> You are gazing at the Light
> With its own ageless eyes.
> (Harvey, *Passion*, 163)

Moving on to the rational God of the Reformation and the still more rationalistic deistic clockmaker of the Enlightenment, Armstrong brings us to the beginning of the nineteenth century and the rise of atheism. The theories of Darwin, Freud, and Nietzsche, combined with the science of Newton and Descartes, left little room for a concept of any sort of real deity existing separate from us. For Nietzsche God was "a crime against life," having through his church denigrated the body and supported a weak moral system (Armstrong, 356). For Freud God was a concept best outgrown.

Yet the deity archetype has refused to die. Carl Jung

rejected Freud's view of God, postulating—if somewhat ambiguously—a mystical god of the individual imagination, one that is really a psychological phenomenon. For many liberal theologians and philosophers, too, the god who emerged in the twentieth century could no longer be a personal being. For Paul Tillich a personal god was an absurdity, "a being among beings" rather than Being (Armstrong, 382–83). For philosopher Martin Heidegger (1889–1976) God was the Nothing that gives rise to existence. For Jewish theologian Martin Buber (1878–1965) God was personal but was discovered in contact with other people. Life itself, then, was an interrelationship with God. Teilhard de Chardin and Thomas Berry, both Catholics, both dedicated to science, prefer to see God in terms of a culmination of the evolutionary process in which existence becomes something like the Hindu concept of Brahman. "The Universe, the solar system, and the planet earth in themselves and in their evolutionary emergence," writes Berry, "constitute for the human community the primary revelation of that ultimate mystery whence all things emerge into being" (quoted in Lonergan and Richards, 107).

For philosopher-anthropologist Gregory Bateson (1904–1980), "The individual mind is immanent but not only in the body. It is immanent also in the pathways and messages outside the body; and there is a larger Mind of which the individual mind is only a subsystem. This larger Mind is comparable to God and is perhaps what some people mean by 'God,' but it is still immanent in the total interconnected social system and planetary ecology" (Bateson, 461).

Karen Armstrong sums up what seems to be the current state of deity formation when she suggests that God cannot exist "in any simplistic sense . . . the very word 'God' is only a symbol of a reality that ineffably transcends it" (397).

However we perceive of deity now in the intellectual sense, it is likely to become neither masculine nor feminine and, therefore, in any human sense nonpersonal as it slowly takes form in our collective psyche. Our evolving vision of a Supreme Being may well be a Brahman-like essence of Being of which we and all things are mysteriously parts and of which all deity myths are partial metaphors, worthy of respect but not exclusive allegiance. Such an entity would speak more clearly than traditional symbols alone to a togetherness not proclaimed by a god but made necessary by evolution and ecology. This is an image of deity that can inspire, even through our existing—albeit reexamined—scriptures, liturgies, and religious traditions, the awe and wonder inspired by so many earlier versions of the same archetype, the awe and wonder felt in the presence of an interconnected dance of creation that is beyond understanding.

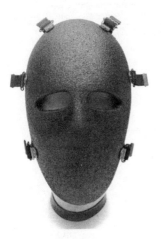

CHAPTER IV

The Hero

Myth, Psyche, Soul,
and the Search for Union

" . . . the wonderful song of the soul's high adventure . . . "

JOSEPH CAMPBELL

Six Hero Myths

Hainuwele

Among the first nine families of the West Ceram people who originally emerged from bananas in the Molucca Islands in what is now Indonesia, there was a dark-skinned night hunter called Ameta, whose dog one night was attracted by the scent of a wild pig. The pig escaped into a pond but drowned. Ameta dragged it out of the pond and was surprised to find a coconut impaled on its tusk. Ameta was sure this coconut must be a great treasure because there were as yet no coconut palms on earth. He wrapped the coconut like a baby in a cloth decorated with a snake figure and took it home. He planted it according to instructions received in a dream and in three days a coconut palm tree had grown to full height. In three more days it blossomed and Ameta climbed it to retrieve some of the fruit. In so doing he cut himself and some of his blood fell on a leaf and mixed with some sap and soon a little face formed and still later a beautiful little girl. The dream messenger instructed Ameta to wrap the girl in the snake-decorated cloth and to bring her home. This he did and was amazed when in a very few days the girl, whom he named Hainuwele, was fully grown and defecating valuable things like bells and dishes.

Soon it was time for the nine families to perform what is called the Maro dance at a place called the Nine Dance Grounds. As always, the women sat in the center of the grounds handing out betel nut to the men, who danced around them in a spiral. Hainuwele sat in the very center. On the first night she, too, handed out betel, but on the second night she gave the dancers coral, on the third fine pottery and on each successive night something still more valuable.

The people became jealous of Hainuwele's wealth and decided to kill her. Before the ninth night's dance they had prepared a deep hole at the center of the ceremonial grounds, and during the dance they edged Hainuwele into the hole and covered her with earth. Ameta soon missed his "daughter," and discovered through his magical skills that she had been murdered during the Maro dance. He immediately took nine pieces of palm leaf to the dance grounds and stuck them into the earth, the ninth one at the very center of the grounds. When he pulled out that piece of palm he found bits of Hainuwele's flesh and hair attached to it. He dug up the body, dismembered it, and buried the pieces, all but the arms, in various places in the dance grounds. Within minutes there grew the plants that are to this day the staples of the Ceramese diet.

Leeming, *Creation Myths*, 43–44

Wanjiru

For three years there was no rain and the earth was dry. The people met in a large open place to dance for rain, but the shaman told them that only by buying the maiden Wanjiru could they cause rain to fall. Each man must return in two days with a goat for her purchase. When the men returned with their goats, the maiden Wanjiru also came with her family. She was placed in the middle of the circle and immediately began to sink into the ground. Both she and her family cried out in dismay, but the goats were given to the family, and as Wanjiru sunk further and further she cried out, "There will be rain." As people tried to save Wanjiru they were paid off with goats. "My own people have done this to me," said Wanjiru as she vanished into the earth. Then the rains came in abundance.

One night a young man much in love with Wanjiru resolved to follow her into the earth. He stood on the spot in the center of the dance circle and sank quickly to a world below. There, after following a long road for some time, he found his lost love and carried her out into our world again. When Wanjiru appeared again at the dance circle the people were amazed. Then the young man married his Wanjiru who had been lost and now was found.

African myth; after Leeming, *World*, 281–83

King Arthur

There are many stories about the mysterious conception and birth of the "once and future king," but little is known about him until his fifteenth year when his father, Uther Pendragon, died and he stood to be King. When opposition developed to his crowning, the archbishop proposed that on Christmas Eve prayers be lifted for some sign from heaven. Miraculously, a stone in which a sword was deeply embedded appeared before the church. On the stone were the words "I am called Excalibur/Unto a king, fair treasure." The nobles agreed that whoever could remove the sword from the rock would be named King. But of all of the warlords, knights, and minor kings who tried to remove it none succeeded, until Pentecost, the feast of the Holy Spirit of God. On that day Arthur arrived at the church in search of a sword to replace the broken one of his foster brother Sir Kay, whose squire he was. Noticing the sword in the rock, he pulled it out easily and took it to Sir Kay. In possession of the sword, Sir Kay thought he could become King, but when doubters demanded that he replace the sword in the rock and then remove it again to demonstrate his kingship he was unable to remove it. When Arthur

once again easily performed the task he was proclaimed King.

after Leeming, *Mythology*, 47

Water Pot Boy

A woman at Sikyatki had a beautiful daughter who
refused to get married. The mother spent her days
making water pots, and one day she asked the daughter
to help mix some clay while she went for water. The girl
put some clay on a flat stone and stamped on it to
smooth it out. Somehow some of the clay entered her
and she became pregnant.

Her mother was angry about her daughter's condition and was horrified when her daughter gave birth to
a water pot boy instead of a regular baby. But the girl's
father was pleased, and he greatly enjoyed watching his
"grandson" grow.

In about twenty days Water Pot Boy was big enough
to play with the other children of the village, who
became quite fond of him. But his mother cried a lot
because he had no arms or legs—just eyes and ears and
a mouth for feeding at the top of the pot.

Soon Water Pot Boy begged his grandfather to let
him go rabbit hunting like other boys, but his grandfather said he couldn't as he didn't have any arms or legs.
The boy pleaded so hard that his grandfather finally
gave in and let his grandson roll along next to him
while he searched for rabbits down under the mesa.

Suddenly Water Pot Boy spied a rabbit and rolled quickly after it out of sight of his grandfather. As he rolled along he hit a large rock and broke and out of the broken pieces sprang a fine boy, beautifully dressed with lots of turquoise, good leather, and feathers. Delighted to be free of his old "skin" and now extremely skillful and fleet of foot, he caught four rabbits before rejoining his grandfather at the foot of the mesa.

Naturally the grandfather did not recognize his grandson. "Who are you?" he asked the boy. "Have you seen my Water Pot Boy?" "That's me!" said the boy, but at first his grandfather didn't believe him. Finally, after the boy explained about the rock the old man accepted him as his grandson and they went home. When they got home the boy's mother thought he was a suitor being brought to marry her and she became upset. But when her father explained that the handsome boy was in fact Water Pot Boy everything was O.K and the boy went off to play with his old friends.

One day Water Pot asked his mother who his father was.

"I don't know," his mother said.

"Well, I'm going to find him."

"You can't—I've never been with a man, so there's no place to look."

"Well, I think I know where he must live," said Water Pot, and after his mother fixed him a pack of dried meat and some water he left, walking southwest toward Horse Mesa Point. There, near a spring, he came upon a man, who asked him where he was going.

"I'm going to see my father," answered the boy.

"You'll never find him," said the man. "Who is he, anyway?"

"I think you're my father," said Water Pot.

Now the man glared at the boy, trying to scare him, but the boy held his ground and stared right back.

"Yes, I am sure you are my father," he said.

Finally the man smiled and embraced the boy and took him over to the spring and then directly into it. Down in the water he found all of his father's relatives, who ran up and hugged him. The next day he left the spring and went back to the village to tell his mother what had happened.

Not long after that, his mother got sick and died, and the boy decided to go back to the spring. There he found his mother down with the other relatives. His father greeted him, revealing that he was Red Water Snake and that he had made the boy's mother die so that she and Water Pot Boy, too, would come over to the spring to live with him. And that's where they still live.

Tewa Indian story
after T. P. Coffin and Leeming, *Mythology*, 26 ff

Kyazimba

The Wachago people of Tanganyika tell how a very poor man—Kyazimba was his name—was determined to find the home of the Rising Sun. After many days of seemingly hopeless journeying he was approached by a little old lady who wanted to know where he was going and why. After he told her he was looking for the home of the Rising Sun, the old woman wrapped Kyazimba in a magic cloak, which took him to the midpoint of the sky, where the Sun stops each day for a feast with his followers. The old woman presented Kyazimba to the Sun and the great being blessed the pilgrim and sent him home to enjoy great prosperity.

after Leeming, *Mythology*, 118

Kutoyis

The Blackfoot hero Kutoyis was born in this way. An old man stole a big clot of blood from the catch of his wicked son-in-law. He and his wife placed the clot in a pot of boiling water to make soup and immediately heard a child crying. Upon opening the pot they found a baby and named it Kut-o-yis, or Bloodclot. The old couple knew that the son-in-law would kill any boy child so they disguised it as a girl. On the fourth day Kutoyis had become a man and soon after he killed the son-in-law before going in search of other evil beings and monsters that tormented the people. He entered the mouth of the great Wind Sucker and killed the beast from within, freeing all the people trapped there. He allowed himself to be killed, dismembered, cooked, and eaten by the great Man-Eater. But each time he was reborn, and finally he killed the Man-Eater.

after Leeming, *World*, 298–304)

THE HERO

Since the days when we believed that deity might actually "come down" to interact with us in the world, human beings have tended to leave God to the theologians and philosophers and to find sources for awe and wonder in heroes, those special fellow humans infused to varying degrees with divine or superhuman qualities. There have always been both religious and secular heroes. Some, to be sure, have been incarnated deities, some have been humans with at least one divine parent, some have derived their power simply from their allegiance to divine purpose, and some have performed seemingly impossible deeds in the name of entities that have nothing to do with religions. Heroes have been fictional and historical. Our heroes reflect our priorities; they are metaphorical representatives in myth of our particular cultural values—personae of our cultural psyches. Moses, Jesus, Muhammad, Theseus, Sir Gawain, and Joan of Arc are heroes to their cultures, as are Frodo, Joe DiMaggio, and Martin Luther

King, Jr. to theirs. As Joseph Campbell has so clearly demonstrated, when we consider these heroes and their myths comparatively, we discover a universal hero myth that speaks to us all and addresses our common need to move forward as individuals and as a species. "The Hero," writes Campbell, "is the man or woman who has been able to battle past his personal and local historical limitations to the generally valid, normally human forms" (*Hero*, 19–20). The essential characteristic of this archetype is the giving of life to something bigger than itself. By definition, the true hero does not merely stand for the status quo; he or she breaks new ground.

THE MONOMYTH

Campbell's study of the hero myth—which relies on Carl Jung, Otto Rank, Lord Raglan, and others who have made comparative studies of the archetype—presents us with what, using a word coined by James Joyce, he calls the monomyth. The hero of the monomyth searches for something lost, and in that process undergoes a series of transformations as significant thresholds are crossed. Three essential elements make up the middle of the monomythic life: the Departure from home, the Adventure in the unknown world, and the Return with some new understanding. These three elements are framed by an appropriate beginning and ending.

The hero life often begins with a miraculous conception and birth. Water Pot Boy is conceived when a piece of clay enters his mother. The Aztec man-god Quetzalcoatl is conceived when God breathes on his mother Chimalman in his form as the "morning." Hainuwele is born of the combination of coconut sap and a drop of blood. In the case of the Buddha, divinity enters the world through the agency of a white elephant in Queen Maya's dream. A clot of blood is the vehicle for the Blackfoot Indian culture hero Kutoyis. Often the hero, the divine child, is born of a virgin. Almost always he or she comes at a time of great need—the darkest night of the cultural year, a time of general suffering.

Even to the most rational among us, conception and birth, like the emergence of spring from winter, are miraculous. In any case, the hope for a new beginning is ubiquitous. We long for the hero who can represent all of us—as a culture, and indirectly as a species—a figure who belongs not to any one family but to all of us. He is conceived and born mysteriously because like the first human—Adam in the Middle East, Kamunu in Zambia, or the Djanggawal in Australia—he springs from the eternal essence. The hero is our second chance. The hidden place—the stable, the grove of trees, the cave— where the hero is born and the painful times in which he emerges remind us that even the gods require the elements associated with the Mother—earth, flesh, pain—to enter the world as one of us. Not surprisingly, the newborn hero is almost immediately threatened by the first of the "guardians at the gate" of the status quo: the kings, jealous fathers, or demons who cannot tolerate the presence of a force for new understanding. Thus Herod sends soldiers to kill any child who might be what the magi have called a new King. And when other magi announce the birth of Zoroaster to King Duransarum, he attempts to stab the child himself. Sigurd and Moses are hidden away for their own protection. The real Water Pot Boy is disguised as a pot until he is ready to break out of childhood into the heroic Departure and Adventure.

As a child the hero must somehow prove him- or herself. Signs of the divine essence must shine through. Krsna, the avatar of the god Visnu, kills a demoness while still in the cradle. The boy Arthur removes the sword from the rock. Theseus retrieves his father's shoes and sword. The Irish hero Cuchulainn, still a mere boy, kills the giant watchdog of Culann. Jesus amazes the Elders in the Temple. As the young wife of the Pāndava brothers in the Indian epic the *Mahābhārata*, Draupadī reveals her inner divinity when, through Krsna's power, the evil Kauravas fail to strip her of her miraculous sari.

Once adulthood is achieved, the hero frequently undergoes a preparatory period of isolation before receiving a call to action, which the hero sometimes initially refuses. Moses the shepherd alone in the fields is called from the burning bush, and his reluctance must be overcome by God himself. The Ojibwa Hiawatha prototype Wunzh is called during his lonely vision quest, but before he can begin his adult journey he must wrestle with the corn god, with divinity itself. Jesus must be tempted in the wilderness, and the Buddha must be tempted by the fiend Mara.

All of these events are preparation for the beginning of the hero journey, the Departure. Like Odysseus, who is reluctant to accept the call of the Greeks to leave wife, child, and possessions to fight in Troy, or like Tolkien's Bilbo and Frodo, who would rather not leave the comforts of Hobbit ways, the hero must leave home precisely because he must break new ground in the overall human journey. The old ways must be constantly renewed and new understandings developed. The Blackfoot Kutoyis must search for monstrous enemies of the people, the Knights of the Round Table must give up the comforts of Camelot to achieve renewal through adventure, and Gilgamesh must leave home to seek eternal life.

The adventure of the hero is marked by several universal themes. The first of these is the search. Sometimes the questing hero looks for something lost. Odysseus's son Telamachos, Theseus, and Water Pot Boy all search for the Father. Gilgamesh, Jason, the Knights of the Round Table, Moses, and the East African Kyazimba seek objects or places—often lost ones—of potential importance to their cultures—the plant of immortality, the Golden Fleece, the Holy Grail, the Land Where the Sun Rises, the Promised Land. More overtly "religious" or philosophical heroes such as the Buddha or Jesus look to less tangible goals: Enlightenment or Nirvana, the Kingdom of God.

The quest always involves difficult trials. There are frightening and dangerous guardians at each threshold the hero must cross. And there are tests. Herakles must perform the twelve labors, the Grail heroes must prove themselves through various deeds and, like heroes of many cultures, are tested by a femme fatale. This enchantress, a particularly popular nemesis of the patriarchal hero—Adam's Eve, Aeneas's Dido, Samson's Delilah—is the archetypal image of the dangerous sexual and merely personal alternative to the true goal.

Many heroes must die and descend to the place of death itself, sometimes as scapegoats for the mistakes of others. Jesus and Osiris die, as do the African heroine Wanjiru and the Ceramese heroine-goddess Hainuwele. In death the hero is planted in the Mother, and during that period of dark gestation confronts the terrors and demons of the underworld.

But the hero returns, usually in the spring. He or she is resurrected, as in the case of Persephone, Wanjiru, Hainuwele, or Jesus. Several of these heroes become sources for material or spiritual food for their people: Osiris emerges from the earth as the god of grain;

Hainuwele's buried limbs become vegetables; numerous Native American corn heroes and heroines become the staple food for their people; for the Christian the resurrected Jesus is the "bread of life." These are all versions of the boon or great gift that the hero brings upon returning from the depths of the quest. Other versions include: the corn culture brought back by the Ojibwa hero from his vision quest; the curing qualities of the Grail brought back by the successful Grail hero; the "Law," brought by Moses; the knowledge of Enlightenment that is the Buddha's gift; the word of God that is Muhammad's; or knowledge of the runes, the result of the Norse god Odin's human and heroic act of hanging himself on the tree.

As an epilogue to the Departure, the Adventure, and the Return, the hero can make a second return, this time to achieve union with the cosmic source of his or her being. Jesus and the Virgin Mary ascend to God, and a legend has it that Abraham did too. The Buddha, King Arthur, and Moses all undergo a kind of apotheosis, a union with the ultimate mystery.

The Patriarchal Hero

It is important to remember that in myths, as in dreams, all of the elements belong to the culture that "dreamed" them. The hero of the myth is, of course, culturally analogous to the Ego or Persona of dream. And the given culture, with the help of experience, tradition, and environment, also dredges up the particular gate guardians, trials, and quest goals. The hero myths we have, those available to us for comparison, are primarily from strongly patriarchal societies, and it is to the patriarchal ur-hero who emerges from these myths that we must look for insight into the collective psyche of our present world, even as we watch for indications of a new hero who might be emerging from the revival of the feminine and the new planetary mythology referred to earlier.

In the traditional patriarchal embodiment of the archetype, the hero's adventures, even when accomplished for the good of all, are dependent on his separateness from us. In the mind-set determined by our hierarchical Sky God bias, as God is above and beyond us, so is mind separate from matter, soul from body, and the hero from us. Even the heroes who live humble lives and preach nonaggressive, nonhierarchical approaches to life's problems—heroes such as Jesus, the Buddha, Ghandi, Martin Luther King, Jr.—are isolated from us, capable of deeds that are, in effect, superhuman. Whether Gilgamesh or a super athlete, the patriarchal hero has powers greater than ours. Although he is necessarily born of a woman, the hero quickly becomes separate from her. The Buddha's mother, like many, almost always humble hero mothers, dies after the birthing function is completed. Mary is told by Jesus that he has more important things to think about than her or his family. Theseus's mother, like King Arthur's, is tricked into intercourse, being little more than a vessel for Poseidon's seed. The patriarchal hero's initiation often involves a violent manly deed, such as the strangling of a monster, or the overpowering of an anti-hero. The quest trial, too, emphasizes physical prowess more often than not, and includes the defeat of death itself. Not surprisingly, the patriarchal myth is a celebration of stereotypically male characteristics, and specifically of male power. Sky God power is transmitted to an earthly son, and the feminine element of life is greatly diminished.

For the most part we can relate to the traditional hero archetype to the extent that we understand the need to succeed, to persevere against seemingly impossible odds. And we can relate to the nationalistic, familial, or ethnic loyalty represented by most of these heroes. These, after all, are values we teach in our schools, homes, legislatures, and places of worship.

Archetypal patterns, however, like individual heroes, can evolve. Secular heroes, for instance, have reflected secular values and understandings of particular eras. The secular world changes more easily than the religious world. T. S. Eliot's Prufrock and Albert Camus' "stranger" are negative representatives, anti-heroes of the age of existentialism, who express a sense of impotence, disillusionment, and the absence of spirituality. It could be argued, however, that Prufrock and the existential heroes of the late nineteenth and twentieth centuries as well as the heroes of popular music and sports today are merely tangents of the old patriarchal myth. Prufrock and the "stranger" would like the old order if they could find it, and the adored singer of violent lyrics remains within the framework of the god of power.

HEROINES AND THE MOTHER WORLD

It would be of interest to know more of the deeds of heroes associated with goddess mythologies predating recorded history—if such mythologies ever existed. It is possible, for instance, that the popular motif in fairy tales of the prince's marriage to the enchanted princess, following the many trials and tests, suggests something of an older pre-femme fatale pattern in which the princess—Campbell calls her the "Goddess-Queen" (*Hero*, 120)—represented life itself. In that case the hero's marriage to her would have signified ultimate knowledge of life.

There is an element of this pattern in the union of the hero and the mysterious Montaño Woman in Leslie Marmon Silko's *Ceremony*, and we discovered earlier that feminine elements remain a powerful force in the matrilineal cultures of the American Southwest.

In the *kinaalda*, the puberty ritual of Navajo and Apache girls, the initiate becomes the creating Goddess Changing Woman herself and attains curative powers for a time. In the Candlemas Buffalo Dance at the Pueblo of San Felipe, a maiden becomes, in effect, heroine for a day when she ascends a mountain barefooted to bring down the Buffalo King and other animal dancers, who in the course of the ceremony that follows symbolically allow their lives to be sacrificed as food for the tribe. The maiden is the only female in the dance and one senses that it is her giving of herself to the Buffalo King that makes the beneficial sacrifice possible. In these rituals we glimpse an older idea of heroism in which the ordinary individual—one of us—can only be recognized as hero in a communal act, a breaking out of the merely personal life into a sacrificing of the individual to the larger communal self. There are remnants of this communal heroism in myths such as those of Hainuwele and the African Wanjiru, each of whom sank into the ground in the middle of a dance ground—itself the sacred symbol of a cultural "world"—and through death brought new life.

It should be noted that in the established religions of our time heroes exist whose values seem as attuned to these hypothetical ancient goddess traditions as to those of their patriarchal cultures. The mildness and humility of Jesus and the Buddha represent attempts to bring growth and change to the older heroic traditions. Both men place less emphasis than their cultures on old patriarchal laws and hierarchy. Both attempt to break down barriers between themselves and their people. But ultimately both fail to defeat the forces in their cultures that would distort their works and words in such a way as to create out of them new hierarchies, new power-based laws of dominance. This is especially so of Christianity, in which Jesus is raised by the institution named after him to the distant level of Son of God seated on a heavenly throne—an institution in which hierarchy and power and splendid palaces and temples early on become the visual symbols of the religion. There was the rise of Mary from folk tradition as a de facto goddess to balance the dominance of traditional male values in the Church. But the church fathers, as noted earlier, repressed much of Mary's earth-based, non-separate nature by emphasizing her virginity and depriving her of sexuality even as she became, through her Assumption, like the old outlawed Asherah, Queen of Heaven, a position clearly separated from ours.

MYSTICISM

There has always been an alternative to the patriarchal vision among people with whom we associate the term "mysticism." It is often said that when mystics of various traditions are placed in a room together, there is little or no disagreement. Ibn al Arabi would have no difficulty accepting the views of Meister Eckhart or the Kabbalists. The Cosmic Christ of Thomas Berry and Matthew Fox is, in effect, celebrated in the poetry and dance of Rumi and his dervishes. And Hindus of the Vedānta tradition, esoteric Buddhists, and Native American worshipers of the Great Mystery would feel comfortable with all the others. Mystics have traditionally worked from established traditions. They have used Judaism, Christianity, Hinduism, Buddhism, Islam, Taoism, Shinto, and so-called Pagan systems as vehicles to move toward a center, to which they have applied many terms. But they have always placed the interrelatedness of all things before exclusivity and local theology. Rather than emphasizing traditional personalities or prophets of the given religion as heroes, they have preferred to emphasize the potential heroism of the individual, the hero adventure of the soul in search of union with ultimate mystery.

Mysticism is frequently undermined by the dominant forces within established religions. Exclusivity, hierarchy, competition, the conquering hero, and especially fundamentalism do not mix well with the inner path. Mystics have always maintained that all religions and their myths are only partial visions of the truth.

Myths of Mystical Union

The Song of Songs

By night on my bed I sought him whom my soul
loveth: I sought him, but I found him not.

I will rise now, and go about the city in the streets, and
in the broad ways I will seek him whom my soul
loveth: I sought him, but I found him not.

The watchmen that go about the city found me: to
whom I said, Saw ye him whom my soul loveth?

It was but a little that I passed from them, but I found
him whom my soul loveth: I held him, and would
not let him go, until I had brought him into my
mother's house, and into the chamber of her that
conceived me.

I charge you, O ye daughters of Jerusalem, by the roes,
and by the hinds of the field, that ye stir not up, nor
awake my love til he please. (Song of Songs, 3:1–5)

The Mouth of Kṛṣṇa-Viṣṇu

At the foot of a banyan tree stood a beautiful boy who
greeted the tired and lonely old sage Mārkaṇḍeya. This
was Viṣṇu as his avatar Kṛṣṇa. "You are tired," he said to
the man. "Find rest in me." Suddenly the man forgot
his cares and looked into the open mouth of Kṛṣṇa. And
a great wind drove him into the mouth. There, inside
Kṛṣṇa he saw the whole universe—streams, people
working, the oceans, the sky. Mārkaṇḍeya walked inside
the boy for one hundred years but never reached the

end of the body. When the wind rose again he was forced out and he found himself once again under the tree with the beautiful boy. "I hope you feel better," said the boy. (*Mahābhārata*)

Once Kṛṣṇa's mother looked into his mouth when he was a child and she too saw and experienced the whole universe, the whole essence of Viṣṇu as Brahman the Absolute. (*Bhāgavata Purāṇa*)

Moses on Mount Sinai

Moses came down from Mount Sinai with the two stone tablets of the Testimony in his hands, and when he came down, he did not know that the skin of his face shone because he had been talking with the Lord. When Aaron and the Israelites saw how the skin of Moses' face shone, they were afraid to approach him. (Exodus 34:29–30)

Jesus on the Mountain

[Jesus] took Peter and John and James and went up a mountain to pray. And while he was praying, the appearance of his face changed, and his clothes became dazzling white. (Luke 9:28–29)

The Miraj (Night Journey)

As Muhammad slept one night—some say near the Ka'bah at Mecca, some say in the house of Umm Hani'—the Angel Gabriel appeared to him and took him on the winged steed Burāq to Jerusalem. There the Prophet met Abraham, Moses, and Jesus and established his primary position by leading the group in prayers. When the mi'rāj, the ladder to heaven, appeared, Gabriel and Muhammad ascended, stopping at each of the seven heavens where Muhammad was identified as Allah's messenger. In the seventh heaven, Paradise, Muhammad approached the throne of God and conversed with him about the rituals of prayer before returning in the morning to Mecca. (after Ibn Ishaq, Sirat Muhammad)

EXTERIOR PILGRIMAGE

Much of the mythology—the imagery of the soul's mystical adventure—is derived from a particular understanding of the rite of pilgrimage, a specific means by which even in the conventional religious context the individual can imitate the hero's journey. A pilgrim is a person who leaves home to travel to an important place with the intention not of staying but of bringing something of spiritual value back into his or her ordinary life. The archetypal connection between the pilgrimage and the hero adventure is clear enough: both are based on the frame of Departure, Adventure, Return, the process of threshold crossing, the achievement of higher knowledge, and even union with the Absolute.

In a sense, the defining characteristic of the human species is its pilgrimage aspect. That is, we are all significant sojourners because we live with the constantly present metaphor of a journey. Of all species, we appear to be the only one concerned with the idea of the Journey of Life. Poets from the Gilgamesh bard and Homer to John Bunyan, Robert Frost, and Jack Kerouac have always explicitly or implicitly celebrated this fact. In the words of Frost's poem "The Road Not Taken," "Two roads diverged in a yellow wood . . . /I took the one less traveled by, /And that has made all the difference."

Behind that metaphor of the Road of Life is our unique human ability to conceive of plot—*mythos*—of what Aristotle defined as narrative with a significant beginning, middle, and end. Ultimately we conceive of our lives that way, and that makes us, at least mentally, pilgrims on a pilgrimage.

The religious pilgrimage is a ritual journey. The pilgrim knows exactly where he is going, exactly what he will find there, and exactly what he is supposed to do once he gets there. The trip can be difficult; it may require discipline, but, as in the majority of such rituals, the most surprising aspect of the journey is the mysterious spiritual and emotional effect particular enactments of rituals can sometimes have. Ritual as used here must be seen in the context of a religious understanding indicated by the Latin word *religare*—meaning to bind back, to re-collect—not only people, but ideas—to make sense of things in the cosmos. What ritual does is to provide the possibility for the individual and/or the community to re-member, to re-create the myth—the sacred story that is essential to the given religion. Almost always, ritual involves some sort of consecrated or sacred space that itself reflects the essential myth. A pilgrimage, then, is a ritual process carried out by pilgrims who, by traveling to a sacred place, renew the power of their culture's sacred narrative in their lives.

The pilgrimage begins with a definitive breaking away from the ordinary—home, everyday concerns, ordinary pursuits. The middle of the pilgrimage is a ritual process clearly defined by the tradition in question. Often it involves seemingly irrational but actually symbolic acts that separate it from the mundane: odd postures; the chanting of strange words, the doing of strange things, the wearing of clothes that in the "real"—or some would say "unreal" world—would be considered bizarre; and, most of all, the dominant presence of a sacred object or place. Hindus journey to Banāres to bathe in the sacred river or they go to other sacred places that they circumambulate, creating a sacred circle of wholeness, or maṇḍala, as they chant sacred words, or mantras. Buddhists visit such sacred places as the Buddha's footprint on Adam's Mount in Sri Lanka or the Bodhi Tree under which the Buddha achieved enlightenment. People of animist traditions frequently see the world itself as a pilgrimage site and live in spaces that symbolize that understanding. The traditional Navajo home, the hogan, with its low, rounded form and its doorway facing east, is built as both a pilgrimage to the Mother as Earth and the Father as Sun. Jews make ritual visits to the old Temple Wall, as they once did to the Temple itself on particular pilgrimage feasts. Christians follow the path of Jesus on the Via Dolorosa, travel to places where the Virgin Mary has appeared to the faithful, or where martyrs gave their lives. For Muslims, the pilgrimage to Mecca—the hajj, specifically to the Ka'bah, the place of the creation, the sacred construct of Ibrahim (Abraham), the place ordained by the Prophet Muhammad as the point toward which prayer is directed—is one of the essential "Five Pillars" of their religion.

Like all religious pilgrims, the Muslim on the hajj imitates the original culture hero and in so doing, in a sense, becomes the hero. Following the last pilgrimage of Muhammad in 632, the faithful Muslim on the hajj leaves the comforts of home, wears special clothes, accepts certain material deprivations, approaches the place that is the center of the universe, and cries out, "Here am I O God, Praise, blessing and dominion are yours, Nothing compares to you, Here am I O God," after which he or she kisses the Black Stone from Heaven itself, performs specific circumambulations, and recites certain prayers. The effect on the pilgrim can be analogous to that on the mythic hero who discovers the ultimate lost object or comes face to face with Ultimate Reality:

> As you circumambulate and move closer to the Ka'bah, you feel like a small stream merging with a big river. Carried by a wave you lose touch with the ground. Suddenly, you are floating, carried on by the flood. As you approach the center, the pressure of the crowd squeezes you so hard that you are given a new life. You are now part of the People; you are now a Man, alive and eternal. . . . The Ka'bah is the world's sun whose face attracts you into its orbit. You have become part of this universal system. Circumambulating around Al-lah, you will soon forget yourself. . . . You have been transformed into a particle that is gradually melting and disappearing. This is absolute love at its peak. (Ali Shariati, *Hajj*, quoted in Armstrong. 156–57)

The return from the hajj or any pilgrimage, like the return of the hero, involves the transference of energy from the sacred place or object to the individual and/or community. We can call that transference healing, enlightenment, re-newal—even recreation, which is, of course, re-creation.

INTERIOR PILGRIMAGE

The words just quoted by the Iranian philosopher Ali Shariati in connection with the exterior pilgrimage that is the hajj suggest another kind of pilgrimage—the interior pilgrimage of the mystic. In an interior pilgrimage the individual, through particular disciplines—meditation, yoga, or contemplative prayer, for example—journeys to the God within. In merging with God, the mystic, like the hero, possesses elements of deity itself. These are the words of the German mystic Meister Eckhardt about the God within to whom he has journeyed:

> God gives birth to the Son as you, as me, as each one of us. As many beings, as many gods in God. In my soul, God not only gives birth to me as his son, he gives birth to me as himself, and himself as me. I find in this divine birth that God and I are the same: I am what I was and what I shall always remain, now and forever. I am transported above the highest angels; I neither decrease nor increase, for in this birth I have become the motionless cause of all that moves. I have won back what has always been mine. Here in my own soul, the greatest of all miracles has taken place—God has returned to God! (quoted in Harvey, *Son*, 282)

Perhaps the primary difference between the interior and exterior pilgrimage lies in the fact that the interior pilgrimage lacks the sense of community that is involved in the exterior pilgrimage. In fact, some might argue that the mystic, like the patriarchal hero, takes on during the interior pilgrimage something of the separateness that makes it difficult for the ordinary human to follow. We think of the ascetic yogi who has no need of visiting any of the sacred cities because through his strict discipline he can visit them all within himself. We think of the Buddha himself under the Bodhi Tree, St. John of the Cross and his "Dark Night of the Soul," or the praying Thomas Merton in the hermitage at Gethsemane. Each of these mystical heroes achieves a state of purity and ecstasy that seems to be beyond us.

Not all mystics practice the lonely journey of the separated hero. Communal ritual can be mystical. For instance, in the "whirling" dance ceremonies of the Mevlevi Sufis of Celaladin Rumi we find a perfect balance between the communal act and the personal. In this ceremony pashas, shoemakers, plumbers, professors, and jewelers—nobles, professionals, and menials alike—dance in planetary togetherness in trance-like personal ecstasy circumambulating love. The center of Sufi being is conveyed in Rumi's words "The dawn of joy has arisen, /And this is the moment of union, of vision" (quoted in Harvey, *Way*, 316).

It is possible to argue—as Victor and Edith Turner

do—that the exterior pilgrimage—the kind taken by the Canterbury pilgrims or the visitors to the Bodhi shrine—is "exteriorized mysticism," a communal ritual attempt to achieve at least momentary union, such as that achieved by the mystics, with the ultimate mystery (Eliade, *Encyclopedia*, 347). For the ordinary human various possibilities for something between exterior and interior pilgrimage as hero journey exist in forms of ritual or liturgy (God's service) in churches, mosques, temples, and other sacred spaces to which long journeys are not required and in which leaders and fellow worshipers contribute to a movement toward the sacred center.

For Christians who follow a strong liturgical tradition, for example, the Eucharist, or Mass, is a mysterious reenactment of the essential myth, that of the pilgrimage undertaken by the culture hero Jesus from birth and baptism to the adventure in search of the Kingdom of God, an adventure that includes death and culminates in the return that is resurrection and the reunion with the "Father" in heaven. The worshiper leaves home, enters the cross-shaped sacred space almost animistically symbolizing the Body of Christ, and, like the hero of old, participates in the mantras, circumambulations, and other ritual actions that are intended to bring him or her to a mystical union with God. Traditionally the Mass moves the initiate from the font of baptism at the western foot of the body to the altar of the sacrificial death and re-membrance in the eastern head where the sun rises. The process is from the darkness of the outer world to the light of the inner.

In Akşehir, near Celaladin Rumi's city of Konya, is a mock tomb that stands as a symbol for the possibility of heroism available to us all. The tomb is of the comic trickster figure Nassredin Hodja, whose ridiculous actions can illustrate the seemingly irrational truths of mystics like Rumi. In front of the typically Islamic gravestone, topped by a turban, is a large gate with a gigantic padlock securing it. We can see that the stone has a little hole in it, from which, presumably, the old teacher can observe the pilgrims who visit his grave. The padlock seems to deny access to the tomb until we notice that the gate stands alone, with no fence attached to it. The pilgrim who would move beyond the merely local to the transcendence of the hodja need only walk around the guardian gate of conventionality and denial.

The Psychological Hero

The mystical understanding has been particularly beneficial to those voyagers willing to walk around the gate, but these pilgrims have inevitably realized the necessity of supplementing the mystical tradition with the myths of their own age, in our case those of psychology and the physical sciences. It is through these myths—the current sources of the awe and wonder needed to experience the mysteries of the universe within and the universe beyond—that the new hero must develop. From the time of Freud, the myths of psychology have given a new dimension to the concept of the inner hero, and the myths of what we have called the New Science corroborate much of what mysticism and psychology have revealed.

It is appropriate to apply the word "myth" to mysticism, psychology, and the physical sciences because each of these approaches to the nature of existence uses hypothetical models and narratives as if they were real, when, in fact, they are metaphors that merely attempt to *convey* reality. The myths of psychology have become for us an important way in which even in common usage we portray what and who we are. For instance, we often speak of the psyche as if it were an actual entity, just as mystics and other religious people have always postulated an actual entity called the soul that inhabits the "inner life" and in some cases can even "fly" away at the time of the body's death. Physical scientists create what they often refer to as "elegant" models and thought experiments such as Schrödinger's Cat or Einstein's Twins to describe otherwise indescribable realities and phenomena. We cannot touch the soul or the psyche or directly experience the thought experiment since they are myths, but as elements of a working vocabulary, as philosophical scaffolding, we accept them as real.

It is to the myth of the psyche and its universal language that we turn in a reexamination of the archetypal hero myth as it is taking form in our age. Even though we recognize that particular hero myths are the stories of cultures and expressions of knowledge at a particular time, we can accept the model of the archetypal hero, who, through the comparative process, emerges in shadow form as a metaphor both for the collective human psyche and for us as individuals. Kṛṣṇa and Gilgamesh as particular expressions of the hero myth are foreign to us, but their common characteristics are not, and through their commonality we can begin to interpret the hero as a central figure who is not separate from us but coincides with our actual internal and even external lives. Ultimately, the unreal worlds of myth, like the unreal world of dreams, reveal psychological truths. We can begin with some more "myths."

Myths of Psychology

Psyche and Soul

The psyche deals with the figures of dreams, the other worlds of fantasy, the movement of thought and feeling and imagination across the levels of consciousness. The psyche's functions are its life. In all its manifold dispositions and indispositions, the psyche consists of the conscious and the unconscious at the meetings of persons in relation, both as individuals and in groups. It is a central fact of human life, perhaps at the very center, even though it has no clear biology and its bodily habitation cannot be clearly fixed . . . . The soul is harder still to locate. . . . Both soul and psyche inhabit the body. (Ulanov, 82, 91)

The Collective Unconscious

The collective unconscious, being the repository of man's experience and at the same time the prior condition of this experience, is an image of the world which has taken eons to form.

That the world has an inside as well as an outside, that is not only outwardly visible but acts upon us in a timeless present from the deepest and apparently most subjective recesses of the psyche—this I hold to be an insight which, even though it be ancient wisdom, deserves to be evaluated as a new factor in building a Weltanschauung.

The [Hero's] ascent signifies a renewal of the light and hence a rebirth of consciousness from the darkness. (Carl Jung, quoted in Frey-Rhon, 122, 125)

THE QUEST FOR SELF

In terms of the psychological myth, the hero journey is that of the conscious mind into the unconscious, the search for the lost self, the ego trapped in a dark world of monsters, temptations, would-be diversions, and roadblocks. Jungian psychology, at least, suggests that to "find" him- or herself the individual must break through to transpersonal and transcultural reality. To achieve individuation or self-identity the individual must not only explore, confront, and sometimes battle personal and cultural demon guardians of the gate, but must find and bring into consciousness the Self imprisoned or denied by those guardians.

The Self is a concept derived from the Upaniṣads of India. It is the *Ātman* or inner expression of Brahman, the Universal Life in everything. The Chandogya Upaniṣad explains it in the famous Parable of the Salt.

Śretaketu was a proud young student of the *Vedas* who failed to answer an essential question posed by his wise father Uddālaka as to the nature of reality. The father asked his son to put a chunk of salt in some water and to report to him in the morning. This his son did, but when his father asked him to retrieve the salt it was clear that it had dissolved. So Uddālaka asked Sretaketu to take a sip from one end of the vessel and to tell him what it tasted like. "Salt," answered the young man. He then asked him to taste the middle and then the other end of the vessel. In both cases the youth tasted salt. Uddālaka ordered his son to

throw away the liquid, but the salt remained salt.
Uddālaka turned to his son and said, "Dear Boy,
you are unable to perceive Being here, but Being *is*
here. This Being is the Self of the entire universe.
This is Reality, this is the Self that is *you*,
Śretaketu. (see Armstrong, 30)

In the tradition of the Upaniṣads, or Vedānta, to
understand and experience this sameness between the
individual's essential being and the universe's being is
the basis of enlightenment or Nirvana. It is the means
by which the individual achieves true herohood, as it
were, which has nothing to do with pride or conquest
but with the realization of one's existence as an embodiment of the transpersonal universe—one's true Self.

In terms of depth psychology, Self is the archetype of
wholeness, that which orders and unifies consciousness
and the unconscious. It is the essence of individuality
and the means by which the identity of a culture and
the species is ultimately expressed. Self can take many
archetypal forms, for which the individual searches in
the process of the inner quest or pilgrimage. God can
refer to the Self, as can the Divine Child or the King.
Christ, the Buddha, or Kṛṣṇa can be an image or symbol of Self and the maṇḍala can be a nonpersonal
embodiment. The fairy tale hero's search for the
princess in the enchanted castle is a search for Self—for
wholeness that is the sacred "happily ever after" mar-

riage of the hero and his psychic energy, or *anima*. Psychologically speaking, Hamlet is a damaged hero who, in order to save himself, must journey into himself to discover kingship and the nature of kingship as Self. Willa Cather's professor in *The Professor's House* realizes that he has ruined his life by betraying the divine child which is not only an embodiment of his youthful ideals but those somehow betrayed by humanity. His difficult quest is a search within for that lost child. In *Four Quartets* T. S. Eliot discovers wholeness in universal symbols for the Self that is a cosmic Christ: "When the tongues of flame are in-folded/ Into the crown knot of fire/ And the fire and the rose are one" (from "Little Gidding"). For Eliot this is a wholeness that can end the seemingly impossible personal and cultural dark night of the soul that had been represented by the personal and cultural "fragments I have shored against my ruin" in "The Waste Land."

A Psychological Monomyth

The psychological hero's life, then, is the search for Self, and we are potentially the heroes of that search. It will be useful to consider the particular steps of the monomyth model in light of our general understandings or myths of the psychological journey. It might be said, for instance, that the hero's miraculous conception and birth speak to the awakening in our adult psychic lives of the imaginative capacities and adventuresome energies of childhood, which can lead us out of the psychic prison and brokenness of adulthood. The development that can follow from such an awakening often involves (as it does for the child hero of myth) the separation from parents and the conventional—one might even say unconscious—duties and activities of the world into which we were born. Indeed, there will be parental influences and social pressures that will work against the call to adventure. The psychological voyager, like the mythic hero, is "the man or woman who has been able to battle past his personal and local historical limitations"(Campbell, *Hero*, 19).

Having accepted the call of the psychic adventure, the psychological voyager departs the ordinary world for a journey into the unknown in search of the lost Self whatever form that Self might take. To be reborn, as it were, the voyager must return to the inner world. As in the case of the mythic hero's journey or the journey of the pilgrim, the passage through the unconscious will involve many significant thresholds blocked by guardians—neuroses, obsessions, and other Self-blocking factors created in the course of one's life. These guardians will demand tests and trials and will have to be fought before each threshold can be crossed, before the true "father" or "mother"—the true essence of what we are—can be attained, before the negative expressions, femme fatales, and shadows of our beings can be replaced by clear and positive projections of our real psychic energy, before that projection or *anima/animus* can be brought to the light of consciousness for the sacred marriage of wholeness.

Many terms have been used to express mythically the seriousness of the journey of depth psychology. Psychologists have variously referred to the Night Journey or the Dark Night of the Soul of the mystics. Joseph Campbell uses the constructs of Freud and those of the Bible—the return to the womb and the biblical Jonah's imprisonment in the belly of the whale—to express the sense of darkness, and hopelessness, but also the possibility of gestation and rebirth, that mark the deepest part of the psychic journey. This is the stage in which we seem to die, to be lost to our old life. To face the monsters and demons of the depths is to face the most frightening forces of our inner world, those we would most prefer to ignore or deny. By now, however, it is perhaps too late to turn back, but it is also difficult to believe in the possibility of continuing. This is the period of existential disillusionment when the journey seems both meaningless and inescapable. It is a period reflected in many great works of literature and film, such as *Crime and Punishment*, "The Waste Land," and *Apocalypse Now*. Jung described his personal version of this stage of the journey and the possibility of moving beyond it:

• It was during Advent of the year 1913 . . . that I resolved on the decisive step. I was sitting at my desk once more, thinking over my fears. Then I let myself drop. Suddenly it was as though the ground literally gave way beneath my feet, and I plunged down into the dark depth. I could not fend off a feeling of panic. But then, abruptly, at not too great a depth, I landed on my feet in a soft, sticky mass. I felt great relief, although I was apparently in complete darkness. After a while my eyes grew accustomed to the gloom, which was rather like a deep twilight. Before me was the entrance to a dark cave, in which stood a dwarf with a leathery skin, as if he were mummified. I squeezed past him through the narrow entrance and waded knee deep through icy water to the other end of the cave where, on a protruding rock, I saw a glowing red crystal. I grasped the stone, lifted it, and discovered a hollow underneath. At first I could make out nothing, but then I saw that there was running water. In it a corpse floated by, a youth with blond hair and a wound in the head. He was followed by a gigantic black scarab and then by a red, newborn sun, rising up out of the depths of the water. Dazzled by the light, I wanted to replace the stone upon the opening, but then a fluid welled out. It was blood. A thick jet of it leaped up, and I felt nauseated. It seemed to me that the blood continued to spurt for an unendurably long time. At last it ceased, and the vision came to an end.

I was stunned by this vision. I realized, of course, that it was a hero and solar myth, a drama of death and renewal (*Memories*, 179)

Should the psychological hero's journey continue, the voyager may hope to break through to a reunion with Self. As the homecoming religious pilgrim bears the marks of spiritual revival and the mythic hero is reborn or resurrected, the psychic voyager who has mastered the inner world of darkness, brings that world, now assimilated, into the light of consciousness. Having achieved at least an element of Self-realization, he or she can move on as a more truly conscious being no longer at the mercy either of conventional lethargy or the negative powers within.

FOUNDATIONS FOR A NEW HERO

In the mythologies of the past the ideal role of human beings has always been represented by heroes. Theseus and Cuchulainn are appropriate heroes for cultures that stress the importance of physical power and are dominated by strong Sky Gods. Wanjiru and Hainuwele are more earth-centered, less concerned with personal success and more willing to fall into the earthly rhythms of life and death appropriate to the Earth as Mother. Although Jesus, the Buddha, and Muhammad represent points of view sympathetic to these earth-centered mythologies, ironically they have all too often been expropriated and assimilated by the old patriarchal value systems. The mystical hero takes up the banner of the lost universal mythology of these heroes, stressing—in contrast to the established religions—values such as inclusiveness and the inner search for a universal, nonmaterial divinity. Psychology has tended to provide modern support for these values.

In twentieth-century science, old absolutes were undermined, the individual psyche was revealed, and a universal interrelatedness was recognized. In the wake of these developments human society is now moving, however awkwardly and violently, toward a more global, planetary culture in which such concepts as nationalism, ethnicity, separate economies, geographically defined ecologies, and the old models of creation and deity that informed and supported these concepts will inevitably be challenged. In this new atmosphere, a fresh mythology of creation and deity is emerging, as are new planetary masks for the universal elements of the hero monomyth, liberating it from quaint museum status, from the misuse of self-serving prophets and movements, and, it must be said, from fundamentalist or exclusionary religions, a process that can already be perceived.

The emergence of a new hero is a complex process

involving several steps both historical and simultaneous. Inevitably the new hero cannot simply slough off the patriarchal hero stories that have clothed the monomyth for several thousand years. These are the stories of Gilgamesh, King Arthur, Theseus, and countless others who assume literary form as the Ahabs, Arjunas, and Rolands so ingrained in our many cultures. But, by the same token, the archetype of the monomyth cannot ignore the realities of the present. As always, the hero is that person willing to break through the merely personal and cultural to universal human revelation. In our time this revelation is one of almost incomprehensible interconnectedness, based on the new knowledge of psychology and the physical sciences and represented by the new mythology.

The Hero Vision of Science and Modernism

As we have seen, this new knowledge emphasizes the necessary role of human consciousness in both personal re-creation and in the larger universal creation itself. In the context of the world as we know it, the potential hero is within each of us and, in a sense, is each of us. Physicist Erwin Schrödinger provides a version of the new mythology and, in so doing, a justification for his Cat in the Box experiment, an experiment that relates

to the necessary function of human consciousness and
the new heroism associated with it:

> You may suddenly come to see, in a flash, a pro-
> found rightness of the basic conviction in
> Vedanta: it is not possible that this unity of
> knowledge, feeling and choice which you call *your
> own* should have sprung into being from nothing-
> ness at a given moment not so long ago; rather
> this knowledge, feeling and choice are essentially
> eternal and unchangeable and numerically *one* in
> all [people], nay in all sensitive beings. But not in
> *this* sense—that *you* are a part, a piece, of an eter-
> nal, infinite being, an aspect or modification of it,
> as in Spinoza's pantheism. For we should then
> have the same baffling question; which part,
> which aspect are *you*? what, objectively, differenti-
> ates it from the others? No, but inconceivable as it
> seems to ordinary reason, you—and all other con-
> scious beings as such—are all in all. Hence, this
> life of yours which you are living is not merely a
> piece of the entire existence but is in a certain
> sense the *whole*; only this whole is not so consti-
> tuted that it can be surveyed in one single glance.
> (quoted in Campbell, *Masks*, 4: 610)

Philosopher of science David Bohm has this to say:

One is led [in the New Physics] to a notion of unbroken wholeness which denies the classical idea of analyzability of the world into separately and independently existing parts. . . . Rather, we say that inseparable quantum interconnectedness of the whole universe is the fundamental reality, and that relatively independently behaving parts are merely particular and contingent forms within this whole. (quoted in Capra, 138)

Here is astronomer Fred Hoyle's view:

Present-day developments in cosmology are coming to suggest rather insistently that everyday conditions could not persist but for distant parts of the Universe, that all our ideas of space and geometry would become entirely invalid if the distant parts of the Universe were taken away. Our everyday experience even down to the smallest details seems to be so closely integrated to the grand-scale features of the Universe that it is well-nigh impossible to contemplate the two being separated. (304)

In the context of an interrelated world such as this, each of us, like the cell in an organism, contains the essence out of which the whole organism—in this case the universe, creation itself—is made. Our particular cellular function would seem to be, as Thomas Berry and others have suggested, to remember or bring the wholeness into the light of consciousness and so to make it real. In his pioneering work on science and literary criticism Herbert Muller has written:

> Nothing is intelligible until it has been grasped as form or structure, nothing is significant until it has been related to other things; science and art alike are an organization of experience, alike establish connections hitherto unperceived or unfelt. In this sense, beauty is truth and truth is beauty; the end of each is the creation of patterned wholes. (35)

In both the scientific and artistic contexts this creation of patterned wholes is essentially a heroic process: the struggle of the hero myth being one between the already formed context or given—the stagnant world the hero is called upon to change—and the re-creative collective mind he or she represents. Our scientific myth-makers provide metaphors for this heroic process, as do our storytellers and artists who, like Virginia Woolf (and her fictional representative Lily Briscoe) stands against the entropic tide in her attempt to capture reality as understood in her time. True artists, of course, have always been the adventurers, the heroes of their time in this sense, struggling against the gate-guarding forces—canvas, stone, the blank page, tradition—that would prevent the miracle of the Bach fugue or the Shakespeare play. In the context of the emerging modern myth, however, in which the struggle between energy events and entropy in an interrelated universe is really the one story we have to tell, it is that story itself—the creative process—that, as we have seen, becomes the subject of art, as it has been from the early twentieth century to the present day.

We might do well to remember William Carlos Williams's little poem, "The Red Wheelbarrow":

So much depends
upon
a red wheel
barrow
glazed with rain
water
beside the white
chickens.

The tension necessary for creation is expressed in the structure of the poem as well as in what it says in the context of that structure. What the poem says or does can only be said or done because of the structure, which is what the poem is about. Insofar as the poem is a metaphor, it represents a new hero "myth" derived from the New Science. The arrangement of the poem might well remind us of the supposition that the structure of space-time depends on the distribution of matter in the universe. In the microcosmic universe that is the poem, energy-carrying words are distributed with originality in such a way as to keep entropy off guard and allow for the most efficient possible transfer of information. Taken out of structural context, the words of the poem are trite and essentially meaningless. "So much depends" on these minor matters for what? But that is the point. The form of the poem is a living example of the essential life-and-death battle between seeing and nonseeing, between consciousness and the denial of consciousness. "Human kind cannot bear very much reality," as Eliot wrote in "Burnt Norton," but "so much depends" on our seeing, even in the conventional barn-yards and wheelbarrows of this interconnected world, the dance of creation. Thus,

> so much depends
>   upon
>   a red wheel

—not a red wheelbarrow. We automatically drift toward what we are used to, but the poet forces us to see a red wheel before we see the expected barrow, and to experience the glazing rain and whiteness before we see the expected water and chickens. By making independent lines of "a red wheel," "glazed with rain," and "beside the white," he turns the expected—even trite—scene into an unexpected vision of earth revealing herself in minor details, reminding us of our role as receivers of information, as direct participants in the creative process. In terms of the old hero myth, the poet draws us into a process by which we achieve a vision of first cause by re-creatively endowing the ordinary with the significance of a larger context.

THE NEW ECOLOGICAL HERO

What mysticism, the Earth Mother vision, psychology, and the modernism of the New Science bring to the hero archetype, then, is a new mask based on what we as a species know at this point in our journey through the labyrinth of existence. What we know is that the old mythologies represented by the old patriarchal and individualistic hero masks are no longer viable as expressions of who and what we are.

In keeping with our monomyth model, we conceive of the birth of the new hero as a miraculous awareness in a dark time of the significance of human consciousness for the life of the planet. Our call to adventure—for we are the heroes of the new myth—is that which is stimulated by our wonder and awe in the presence of the interrelated cosmos revealed to us by mysticism, psychology, and the new understandings of the physical sciences. In the initiation process of the patriarchal hero, the experience of awe and wonder needed to initiate adventure came from a distant God above and His creation. In the new myth—learned from the introspection of the religious heroes alone under the Bodhi Tree or in the wilderness, from the great mystics, and from the philosophers of the psychiatric couch or the observatory—awe and wonder come from the contemplation of a God of which each of us is a part, from the vast intricacy of the unconscious world and creation itself, and from an understanding of the remarkable role of the individual and collective consciousness in the ever-expanding, tightly packed universe.

The new mythology does not create conquering heroes but rather seekers after the transpersonal Self of the Gaian world. We are either heroes of the new myth or captives of the old. Those who refuse the call, who hang on desperately to the dying gods and myths of past value systems, will continue to endanger the world with their blindness to reality. Those who answer the call will depart from the status quo and join those planetary universalists in a breaking away—as heroes have always done—from the merely individual, the merely local, so as to become truly human. These adventurers will confront the guardians at the gates of progress and new understanding—those powers who would protect the nation-state, patriarchal exclusionary religion, and corporate power at all costs. In so doing, the ecological hero will have to endure a dark night of the soul, a perilous journey among the demons that haunt us as a species. As it has always been for heroes, this adventure is a quest for something lost. The universe that science shows us is an elegantly integrated and interrelated universe, an ecological planetary world in which the heroes of exclusionary religions, ancient absolutes, national entities, and political philosophies become the outdated carriers of racism, pollution, corporate greed, war, and disease. The crucial salvation now is communal salvation; without it our species will die and creation will lose its consciousness. It will be the role of the new hero—potentially existing in all of us—to lead the way to the formations of belief systems and ways of thinking that will celebrate and be in accordance with the miracle of the ecological universe. As Campbell has said, "The modern hero-deed must be that of questing to bring to the light again the lost Atlantis of the coordinated soul . . . of rendering the modern world spiritually significant" (*Hero*, 388).

For those who persevere there will be the great boon of this spiritual significance to bring back, a new understanding of a reborn transpersonal Self: "It is by engagement with the universe process," writes historian Caroline Richards,

> that humans discover the truth about who they are. Indeed, the human is precisely that being in

whom the natural world reflects on itself. There is no suggestion of an inherent incommensurability between natural processes and our human apprehension of them. Such a dichotomy makes no sense, since reason—or more broadly, human consciousness—is integral to the emergent cosmic process. (quoted in Lonergan, 97)

Thomas Berry writes of the boon as essential knowledge potentially available to us all:

If humans have learned anything about the divine, the natural or the human, it is through the instruction received from the universe around us. Any human activity must be seen primarily as an activity of the universe and only secondarily as an activity of the individual. In this manner it is clear that the universe as such is the primary religious reality, the primary sacred community, the primary revelation of the divine, the primary subject of incarnation, the primary unit of redemption, the primary referent in any discussion of reality or of value. For the first time the entire human community has, in this story, a single creation or origin myth. (quoted in Lonergan, 37)

The representations of the new hero are still taking shape. In this study we have seen elements of the new hero in writers of high modernism like Virginia Woolf and William Carlos Williams. From the so-called post-modern period we considered the novel *Ceremony* by Leslie Marmon Silko. In that work the hero finally accepts the call to adventure, leaves the corrupt world that had nearly destroyed him, and moves through a complex curing process until, as a new planetary and ecological hero, he is able to discover the Self—his own and that of his species—that had long been lost:

> At that moment in the sunrise, it was all so beautiful, everything, from all directions, evenly, perfectly, balancing day with night, summer months with winter. The valley was enclosing this totality, like the mind holding all thoughts together in a single moment. (237)

This is the modern hero's Holy Grail, the Golden Fleece, the land of the rising sun, the promise of eternal life.

Bibliography

Armstrong, Karen. *A History of God*. New York: Alfred Knopf, 1993.

Artigas, Mariano. *The Mind of the Universe: Understanding Science and Religion*. Philadelphia: Templeton, 2000.

Barbour, Ian G. *Issues in Science and Religion*. New York: Prentice-Hall, 1966.

———. *Religion in an Age of Science*. San Francisco: Harper, 1990.

Baring, Anne, and Jules Cashford. *The Myth of the Goddess: Evolution of an Image*. New York: Viking, 1991.

Basham, A. L. *The Wonder that was India*. London: Sidgwick and Jackson, 1954.

Bateson, Gregory. *Steps to an Ecology of the Mind*. New York: Ballantine Books, 1972.

Berman, Morris. *The Reenchantment of the World*. Ithaca, NY: Cornell University Press, 1981.

✓ Blackburn, Simon. *Think*. Oxford: Oxford University Press, 1999.

Bowker, John, ed. *The Oxford Dictionary of World Religions*. New York: Oxford University Press, 1997.

Campbell, Joseph. *The Hero with a Thousand Faces* (1949). Princeton, NJ: Princeton University Press, 1972.

———. *The Masks of God*, 4 Volumes (1968). New York: Viking Press, 1970.

———. *Myths to Live By*. New York: Viking Press, 1970.

———. with Bill Moyers. *The Power of Myth*. New York: Doubleday, 1988.

Capra, Fritjof. *The Tao of Physics*. San Francisco: Shambhala, 1975.

Coffin, T. P., ed. *Indian Tales of North America*. Philadelphia: American Folklore Society, 1961.

Davies, Paul. *The Mind of God: The Scientific Basis for a Rational World*. New York: Simon & Schuster, 1993.

———. ed. *The New Physics*. New York and Cambridge: Cambridge University Press, 1989.

Davies, Paul, and John Gribbin. *The Matter Myth*. London: Penguin, 1992.

Del Re, Giuseppe. *The Cosmic Dance: Science Discovers the Mysterious Harmony of the Universe*. Philadelphia: Templeton, 2000.

Doty, William C. *The Study of Myths and Rituals*. Tuscaloosa: University of Alabama Press, 1986.

Downing, Christine R. *The Goddess: Mythological Images of the Feminine*. New York: Crossroad, 1981.

✗ Eliade, Mircea. *Myth and Reality* (1962). New York: Harper & Row, 1963.

———. *The Myth of the Eternal Return* (1949). Princeton, NJ: Princeton University Press, 1965.

———. *Patterns in Comparative Religion* (1958). Cleveland, OH: Meridian, 1963.

———, ed. *The Encyclopedia of Religion*. New York: Macmillan and Free Press, 1987.

———. ed. *Essential Sacred Writings from Around the World* (1967). San Francisco: HarperSanFrancisco, 1977.

Eliot, T. S. *The Complete Poems and Plays*. New York: Harcourt, Brace, 1952.

Fox, Matthew. *The Coming of the Cosmic Christ*. San Francisco: HarperSan Francisco, 1988.

———. *Sins of the Spirit, Blessings of the Flesh*. New York: Harmony Books, 1999.

Freud, Sigmund. *Totem and Taboo*. New York: Moffat, Yard, & Co., 1918.

Frey-Rohn, Liliane. *From Freud to Jung*. New York, Putnam's, 1974.

Greene, Brian. *The Elegant Universe*. New York: W.W. Norton, 1999.

Gribbon, John. *In Search of Schrödinger's Cat*. New York: Bantam, 1984.

Griffiths, Sian. *Predictions*. Oxford and New York: Oxford University Press, 1999.

Harvey, Andrew. *Son of Man: The Mystical Path to Christ*. New York: Tarcher/Putnam, 1998.

———. *The Way of Passion: A Celebration of Rumi*. Berkeley: Frog Ltd., 1994.

Hoyle, Fred. *Frontiers of Astronomy*. New York: Harper, 1955.

Jung, Carl Gustav. *Answer to Job* (1954). Cleveland, OH: Meridian, 1960.

———. *The Archetypes of the Collective Unconscious* (1934/54). Princeton, NJ: Princeton University Press, 1959.

———. *Memories, Dreams, Reflections*. New York: Vintage, 1963.

———. *Modern Man in Search of a Soul*. New York: Harcourt, Brace and World, 1933.

———. *Symbols of Transformation* (1956). Princeton: Princeton University Press, 1976.

———. *The Undiscovered Self*. New York: Mentor, 1957.

Leeming, David A. *Mythology: The Voyage of the Hero*, 3rd ed. New York: Oxford University Press, 1998.

———. *The World of Myth*. New York: Oxford University Press, 1990.

———. "To the Lighthouse: A Modern Creation Story." *LIT*, 3, 1992, 205–20.

———. and Margaret Leeming. *A Dictionary of Creation Myths*. New York: Oxford University Press, 1995.

———. and Jake Page. *God: Myths of the Male Divine*. New York: Oxford University Press, 1996.

———. *Goddess: Myths of the Female Divine*. New York: Oxford University Press, 1994.

———. *The Mythology of Native North America*. Norman, University of Oklahoma Press, 1998.

Lonergan, Anne, and Caroline Richards. *Thomas Berry and the New Cosmology*. Mystic, CT: Twenty-Third Publications, 1988.

Lovelock, James E. *Gaia: A New Look at Life on Earth*. New York: Oxford University Press, 1979.

Merton, Thomas. "Symbolism: Communication or Communion?" *New Directions 20*. New York: New Directions, 1968, 1–12.

Mitchell, Stephen, trans. *Tao Te Ching*. New York: Harper and Row, 1988.

Muller, Herbert. *Science and Humanism*. New Haven, CT: Yale University Press, 1943.

O'Flaherty, Wendy Doniger. *Hindu Myths*. Harmondsworth, England: Penguin, 1975.

The Oxford Study Bible. New York: Oxford University Press, 1992.

Raglan, Lord Fitzroy. *The Hero: A Study in Tradition, Myth, and Drama* (1937). New York: Vintage, 1966.

Rank, Otto. *The Myth of the Birth of the Hero* (1936). New York: Knopf, 1959.

Read, Herbert. *The Philosophy of Modern Art*. London: Faber & Faber, 1953.

Richter, Harvena. *Virginia Woolf: The Inward Voyage*. Princeton, NJ: Princeton University Press, 1970.

Shariati, Ali. *Hajj*, trans, Laleh Bakhtiar. Tehran, 1988.

Silko, Leslie Marmon. *Ceremony*. New York: Viking Penguin, 1977.

Stannard, Russell, ed. *God for the 21st Century*. Philadelphia: Templeton, 2000.

Stevens, Wallace. *Poems of Wallace Stevens*, ed. S. F. Morse. New York: Vintage, 1959.

Swimme, Brian. *The Universe Is a Green Dragon: A Cosmic Creation Story*. Santa Fe, NM: Bear & Co., 1984.

Ulanov, Ann, and Barry. *Religion and the Unconscious*. Philadelphia: Westminster Press, 1975.

Watts, Alan. *The Spirit of Zen*. New York: Grove, 1958.

Weigle, Marta. *Creation and Procreation: Feminist Reflections on Mythologies of Cosmogony and Parturition*. Philadelphia: University of Pennsylvania Press, 1989.

Williams, William Carlos. *Collected Earlier Poems*. New York: New Directions, 1951.

Woolf, Virginia. *To the Lighthouse*. New York: Harcourt, Brace, and World, 1927.

Yeats, William Butler. *The Collected Poems of W.B. Yeats*. New York: Macmillan, 1956.

Zimmer, Heinrich. *Myths and Symbols in Indian Art and Civilization* (1946). Princeton, NJ: Princeton University Press, 1972.

Text Credits

from *God: Myths of the Male Divine* by David Leeming and Jake Page. Copyright © 1996 by David Leeming and Jake Page. Reprinted by permission of Oxford University Press. "Ala" and "Ua Zit" and from *Goddess: Myths of the Female Spirit* by David Leeming and Jake Page. Copyright © 1994 by David Leeming and Jake Page. Reprinted by permission of Oxford University Press. "Kyazimba" from *Mythology: The Voyage of the Hero* by David Adams Leeming.. Reprinted by permission of Oxford University Press. "Wanjiru," "King Arthur," "Waterjar Boy," and "Kutoyis," from *The World of Myth* by David Leeming. Copyright © 1990 by Oxford University Press. Reprinted by permission of Oxford University Press.

Excerpts from the Oxford Study Bible edited by M. Jack Suggs, Katharine Doob Sakenfeld, and James R. Mueller. Copyright © 1992 by Oxford University Press. Reprinted by permission of Oxford University Press.

Silko, Leslie Marmon. Excerpt from *Ceremony*. Copyright © 1977 by Leslie Marmon Silko. Reprinted by permission of Viking Penguin a division of Penguin Books USA Inc. and the author.

Stevens, Wallace. Excerpt from "The Idea of Order at Key West" from *Poems of Wallace Stevens*. Reprinted by permission of Vintage a division of Random House.

Williams, William Carlos. "The Red Wheelbarrow" from *Collected Earlier Poems of William Carlos Williams*. Reprinted by permission of New Directions and the Estate of William Carlos Williams.

Yeats, W. B. "Leda and the Swan" from *The Collected Works of W. B. Yeats Volume I: The Poems,* revised and edited by Richard J. Finneran. Copyright © 1928 by Macmillan Publishing Company, © renewed 1956 by Georgia Yeats. Reprinted with permission of Simon & Schuster and A. P. Wyatt Ltd. on behalf of Michael Yeats. Abraham, 123, 132

Index